An Older Adult's Guide to the Internet & E-Mail

Second Edition

Diane L. Martin

Escribe Publishing Inc.

DISCLAIMER

While Escribe Publishing takes great, care to ensure the accuracy and quality of these materials. All material is provided without any warranty whatsoever, including but not limited to, the implied warranties of merchantability or fitness for a particular purpose. Readers are advised that references to third-party websites and online resources do not denote in any way the publisher's endorsement.

Please send all inquiries to:

Escribe Publishing Inc.
244 Fifth Avenue, Suite 2337
New York, NY 10001

ISBN-10: 069257445X
ISBN-13: 978-0692574454
Library of Congress Catalog Number: 2015918645

Dedication

To older adults everywhere who are yearning to join the information age,
Come out, come out wherever you are.

To Herbert R. Martin Sr.
The coolest Dad and cyber-senior I know.

To the many older adults I have had the pleasure of teaching,
many thanks for making my job an absolute joy.

Acknowledgements

I would like to take this opportunity to acknowledge the support and encouragement of LaToya Trowers, Judy Ganeles, Sharon Cunningham, Rajasekhar Vangapaty, George Rosales, and Anahu Guzman. Each of you has made the writing of this book possible.

Learn Microsoft Windows

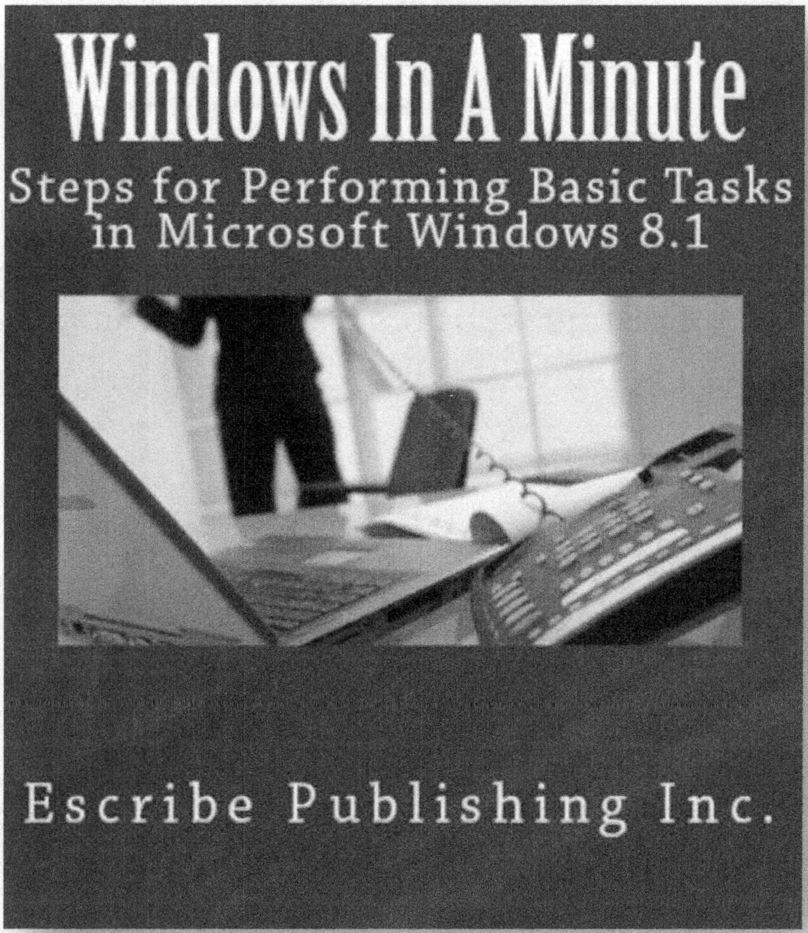

http://www.escribepublishing.com

It's Never too Late to Join The Information Highway

Learning to use the Internet, e-mail, and word-processing programs are critical skills necessary for interacting with businesses, government agencies, family, friends, and colleagues.

See our list of interesting websites for older adults in Appendix B.

The Importance of Computer Literacy

1. **Improving computer literacy can reduce the isolation that comes from being unable to communicate electronically with friends and family.**

2. **The ability to interact effectively with a personal computer is increasingly necessary as businesses, government agencies and the private sector either requires Internet-based contact or makes products and services available exclusively via the Internet.**

3. **Computer usage among older adults can contribute to greater self-esteem and a sense of relevance.**

4. **Using a personal computer for i.e. research, correspondence or budgeting for example is mentally stimulating.**

Contents

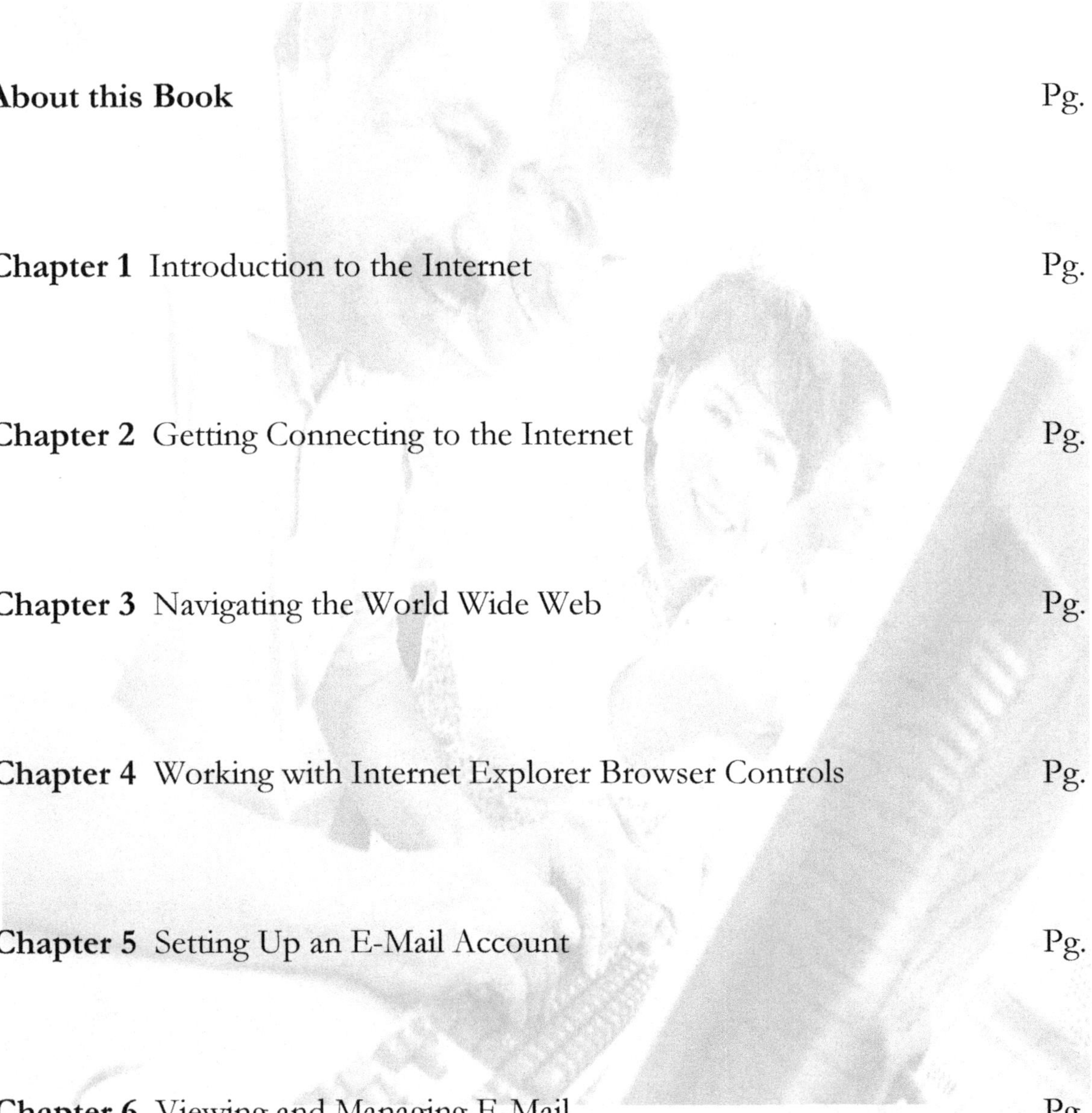

Appendices Pg. 71

Short Table of Contents

Short Table of Contents

About This Book

This book was written as a response to those of you who are still scratching your heads and wondering about this thing called the Internet. Take heart, the fact is that there are still literally thousands of people all over the world, who either do not have Internet access or do not understand what or how the Internet actually works. I am talking about the population of older adults who seem to have missed the information age. Many of you may not have had jobs that gave you a ticket to ride the information highway, or maybe you retired from the workforce as personal computers were becoming so ubiquitous. Whatever the case, whatever the reason, you have probably felt a little isolated from the wonders of the virtual world.

I know older adults who shake their heads in amazement as their children or even grandchildren talk of texting, tweeting, e-mail and e-mail. They wonder how they managed to survive without an e-mail account, but the truth is they really want to be part of it all. They want to read e-mail from their friends, tweets from the grandchildren, and they want to see all those family pictures someone posted on this thing called Facebook.

This book is for all you grandmas, grandpas, aunties, and uncles who finally want to know what is going on. I have included pictures, directional arrows, large type, practice exercises, and notes pages to make using this book as easy as possible.

This is the Internet and e-mail made simple, and it's just the basics. I've pulled back the curtain, I'm telling the secrets, and I'm giving you your ticket to ride. Fasten your seatbelts; it's going to be a bumpy, but amazing ride.

Diane

We are still in the very beginnings of the Internet."

Jimmy Wales

Founder of Wikipedia

That grand encyclopedia of the Internet

Chapter 1

Introduction to the Internet

- Explain the History of the Internet
- Distinquish Between LANs and WANs
- Describe the Advantages of Networking Computers
- Describe the Services Available on the Internet

What is This Thing Called the Internet?

I have found that in explaining what the Internet is all about, it is useful to talk a little about its history. A little is all you really need to know. The Internet actually came into being during the 1960s through the Advanced Research Project Agency. Put simply, ARPA developed a network technology, which enabled computers to transmit, route and receive electronic data in packets that could be disassembled, and reassembled from their source to their destination.

The beauty of this "packet-switching" technology is that chunks of data from different sources could comingle on the same transmission lines, making it possible for many people to use the same lines at the same time. Moreover, ARPA also discovered a method for getting dissimilar networks and computers to communicate using a protocol referred to as Transmission Control Protocol/Internet Protocol or TCP/IP for short. This protocol is really all about the rules networked computers use to communicate with one another.

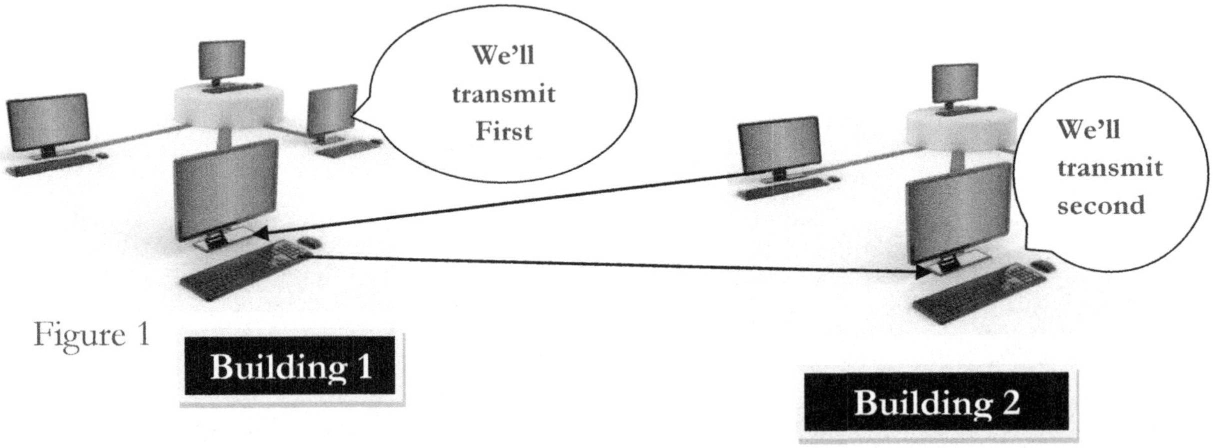

Figure 1

While this kind of information makes computer geeks giddy, don't you worry, packet switching technology and TCP/IP is generally invisible to you. In other words, it is not something you have to give much consideration.

What you may appreciate however, is that beyond its military application in protecting the government's computers, it became apparent during the 1980s that these technologies together could help organizations share information regardless of their location or the type of computers they might have.

LANs, WANs and Wonder

There is one more concept you may appreciate knowing as it relates to the Internet. The technology that made the Internet possible in many ways changed the way organizations do business. Before the advent of the Internet, companies who sought to computerize their operations went out and purchased computers for their employees. During the 1980s personal computers became more prolific. However, those computers were not necessarily connected to each other.

If for example, Imelda in the payroll department wanted to send a communication to Jack in marketing, she would have to type a memo, and place it in an interoffice envelope. Someone in the mailroom would pick up the envelope and within a day or two, it is physically delivered to Jack. Each person was constrained by the time required to communicate the necessary information. In fact, today we refer to non-electronic mail as "snail mail."
Information sharing was fairly limited until LAN technology came along.

What is a LAN?

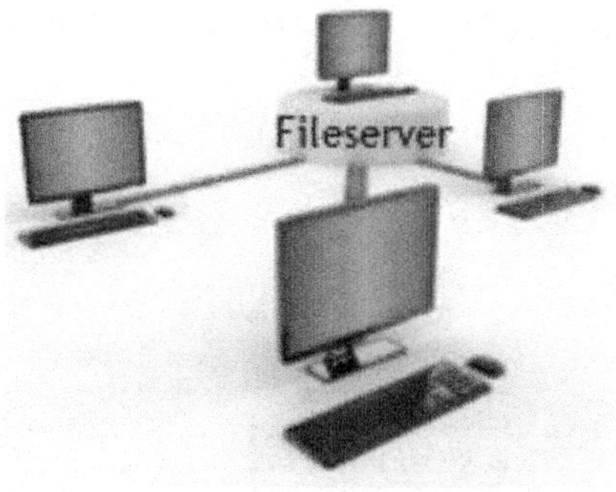

The word LAN is an acronym that stands for **L**ocal **A**rea **N**etwork. A LAN consists of a group of computers within the same building or floor of a building that are connected or networked. This networking is accomplished using fiber optic cable. However, early LANs employed the use of twisted pair telephone cable very much like that found in your home to connect personal computers.

One computer designated as a "Server" is used to control access to the network, regulate traffic and distribute or "serve files" to everyone whose computer (often referred to as a "client") is connected to the LAN. Those files stored on the fileserver's hard-drive may be software like Microsoft Office, individual documents, e-mail programs or other software applications. The fileserver distributes copies of these applications to each user on the network.

A wide area network (WAN) in contrast is a network that extends beyond a single building. The distinction between a LAN and a WAN is really one of geography. WANs rely on transmitting data using high speed telephone lines. Many organizations lease these lines from their local telephone companies.

The Advantages of Networking Computers

The advantage of LAN and WAN technology is that among other things, their use facilitates information sharing. In general, networks make it possible to:

- Allow computers to share files with other computers
- Reduce costs by allowing the sharing of devices, such as printers
- Provide security by controlling access to networked computers
- Communicate more efficiently through e-mail

Remember Imelda and Jack? If each of them worked for an organization in which there was a LAN, Imelda, could send Jack an electronic message without having to leave her desk. Both employees can share a single printer, thus, reducing the cost of each of them requiring their own printer. The Human Resource (HR) director can share information with payroll without physically walking to the payroll department or relying on the office mailroom. If the payroll manager happens to be in California, and the HR director is in New York, both can nevertheless exchange documents electronically through the office WAN. This is rather simplistic; however, to understand this concept, examine the graphic in Figure 2 below.

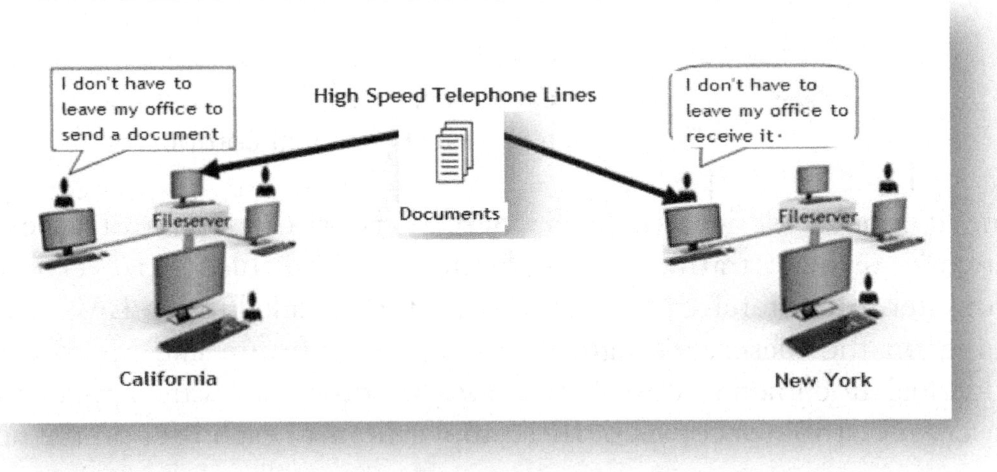

Figure 2

The Power of the Internet

The Internet can be said to be a world-wide network of networks. This is the reason it helps to understand LANs and WANs. Now that you do, let's discuss a little more about why the Internet has become so popular.

During the 1980s research institutions, colleges and universities began to appreciate the ability to share information with one another. In the interest of science and education, the National Science Foundation, (NFS) played an important part in this process by absorbing ARPAnet and building what came to be known as NFSnet. NFSnet became popular and before long, government, industry and the academic community sought to connect to the NFSnet backbone. It's all so amazing don't you think?

Imagine the ability of colleges to share research information with industry, or the government's ability to share information with academia just by making the information electronically available on its fileservers. By the 1990s nearly every sector of our society sought to join the Internet.

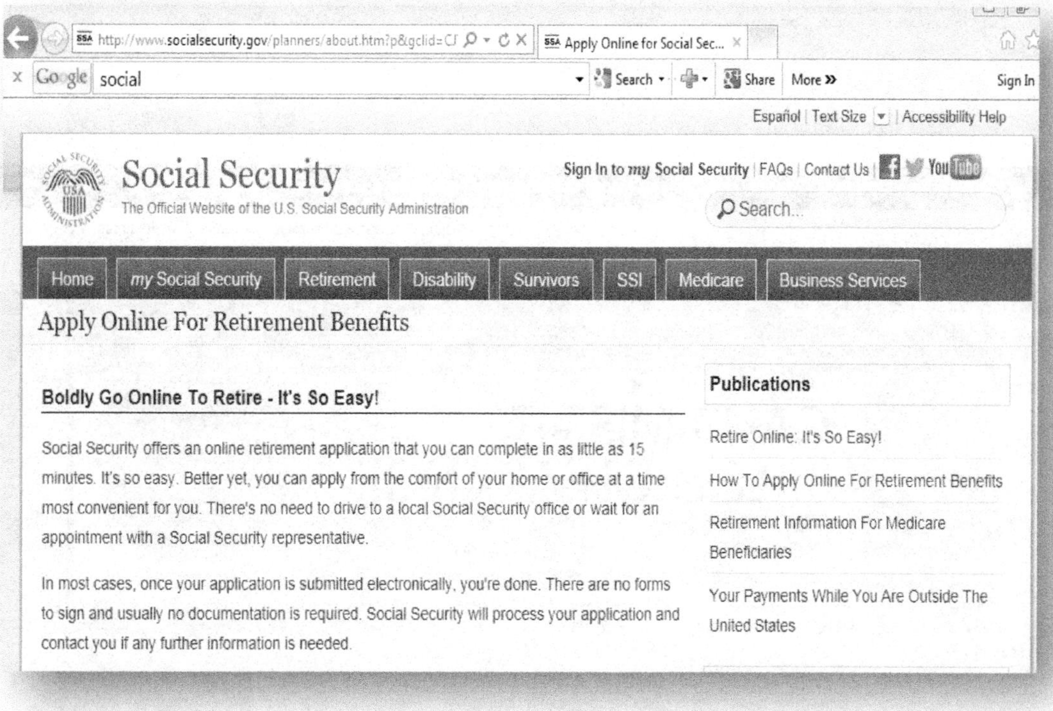

Figure 3

Today almost, every government agency has a presence on the Internet.

Thousands of individuals and organizations have chosen to connect to the Internet. In fact, some sources estimate that there are more than two billion Internet users world-wide. That is a lot of people to market to, and industry has long taken notice. For this reason, new approaches to marketing and advertising followed the development of the Internet as we know it. An entire discipline has emerged on college campuses devoted to something called E-commerce, which is short for electronic commerce.

If you don't feel like marching down to the mall, but you want to pick up a little gift for your niece, you can actually sit in the comfort of your home and do what's called surf (or search) the Internet for a virtual version of your favorite store. For example, Macy's has bricks and mortar stores, but it also has a "Virtual store" where customers can purchase merchandise as we like to say "online". See Figure 4 below.

Figure 4

Your favorite store likely has a "virtual" presence on the Internet.

Let's summarize for a moment. So far you have learned how networks are created, what the Internet is, how it came into being, and a little bit about how various organizations and government agencies are using the internet to engage in e-commerce or provide information to the public. However, that's just the tip of the iceberg. Consider how the wonders of the Internet make it possible for individuals to do such things as:

- E-mail friends and family
- Find and purchase goods and services
- Download your favorite music
- Research the symptoms of an illness
- Find recipes
- Find people, i.e. classmates, relatives, and old friends
- Share photos with family and friends through social media sites
- Buy books online
- Read books and/or the daily news online
- Attend college classes without leaving home
- Show and sell your home
- Book vacations
- Correspond with government agencies

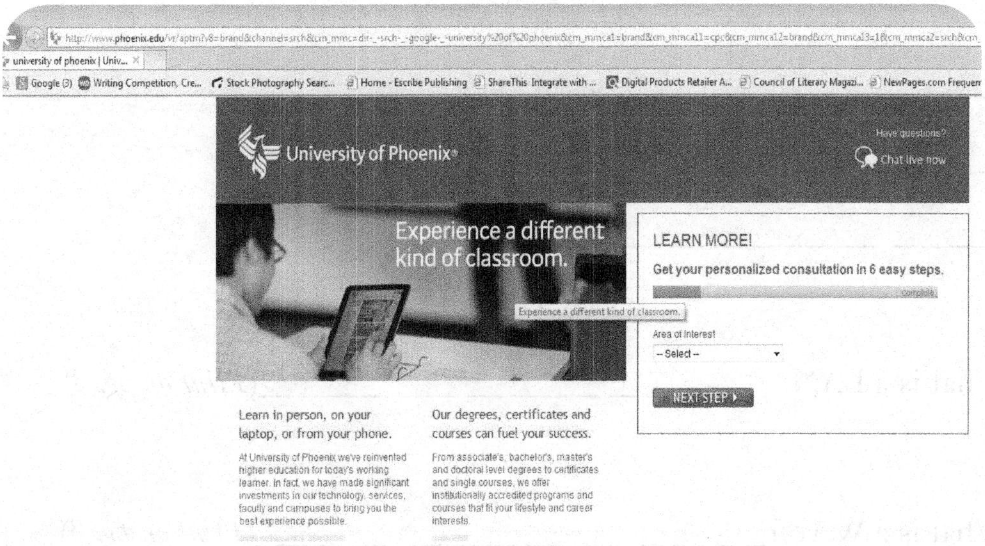

Figure 5

You really can attend college classes in your pajamas.

Chapter Review Questions

1. In the space write down three benefits of computer networks. (*Hint on pg. 4*)

a.__________________________________

b.__________________________________

c.__________________________________

2. What is the term used to describe the selling and marketing of goods online?________________________________.(*Hint on pg. 6*)

3. What kinds of activities can be performed using the Internet? List at least five. (*Hint on pg. 7*)

a.__________________________________

b.__________________________________

c.__________________________________

d.__________________________________

e.__________________________________

4. What is a LAN? ______________________________(*Hint on pg. 3*)

5. What is a WAN?______________________________(*Hint on pg. 3*)

My Notes:

My Notes:

Chapter 2

Connecting to the Internet

- Explain the Requirments for Connecting to the Internet
- Describe How Internet Service Providers Work
- Identify an Internet Address
- Use an Internet Browser
- Identify Domain Names

How Do You Get Connected to the Internet?

Think of the Internet as a global network of networks. This means that in order for you to connect to the Internet it will first be necessary for you to join an existing network.

Fortunately, there are a number of companies whose sole reason for being is to assist a willing customer with jumping on board the information highway. These companies are called Internet service providers or ISPs for short. An ISP has its own network and generally for a fee, they will agree to provide you with an account and connect you to their network making it possible for you to access the Internet. Before you can access the Internet, it will generally be important for you to have:

- A personal computer (Outfitted with a Network Interface card)
- A phone connection (unless you're using a wireless device)
- A router (generally supplied by the ISP, or you can buy your own)
- An Internet service provider (ISP)
- An Internet browser program

Some Internet service providers will dispatch someone to your home to connect a router, jack, and a special cable to your computer. The router they install will handle the connection and data between your computer and the ISP's network. Access to the Internet can also be accomplished through wireless connections. Wi-Fi (wireless) devices like many of today's laptops, tablets, and smart phones rely on radio waves and so-called "hotspots for connectivity rather than actual cables. See the Glossary to learn more about this.

Figure 6

An Internet Service Provider Connects You to the Internet.

Your ISP will provide you with an account or subscription to their service. To access the Internet through your ISP you will need to create a username and a password. Your username identifies you on the ISP's network. Your password authenticates your identity. Usernames and passwords are like bacon and eggs. Where you see one, you can generally expect to see the other.

Once you have established your identity by typing in your username and password a Web page will be displayed. Examine the website in Figure 7.

Working with a Browser Program

To successfully navigate the Internet, you will need something called a browser. A browser is a special software application. Browsers make it possible to view and open hypertext links located within a given web page. For example, examine Figure 7 below. This is a page for a company called Yahoo. This web page contains graphics, text and links to other pages. Notice on the left there are various links such as Mail, News, Finance, etc. If you click on any of the hyperlinks, you will jump to another Web page.

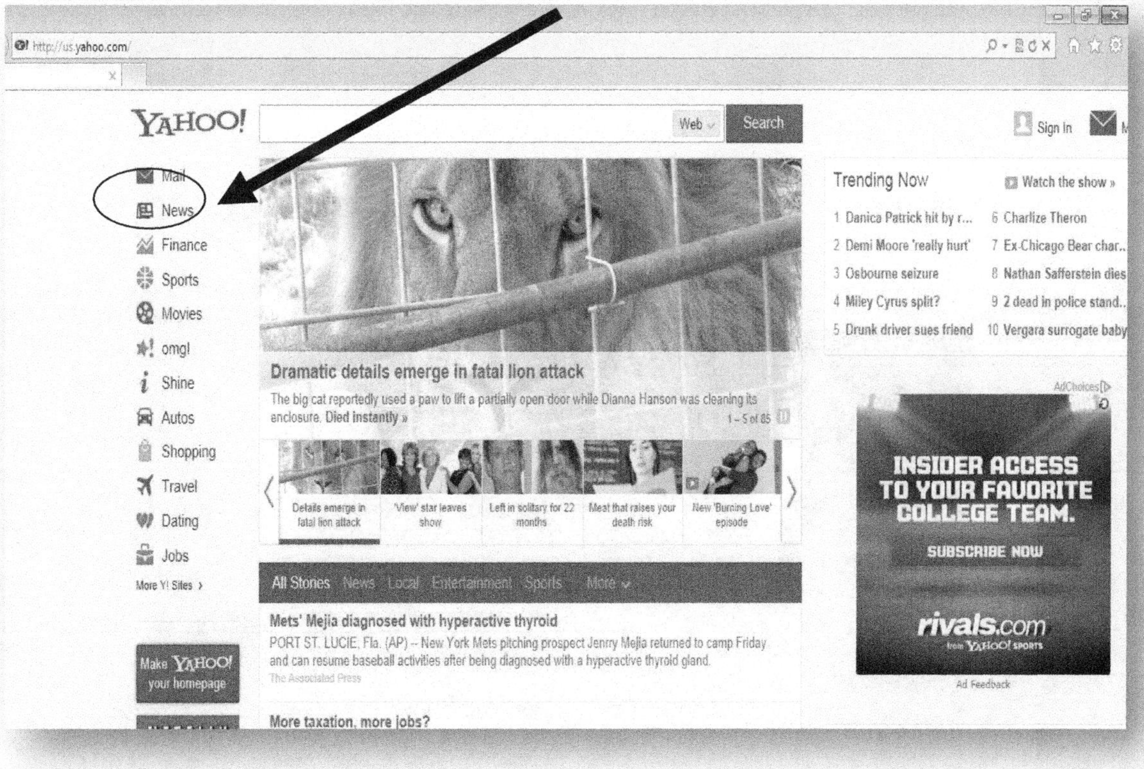

Figure 7

Internet Explorer, developed by Microsoft is an example of a very popular browser program. Without a browser program, searching the Internet would not be very pleasant. The combination of graphics, text, and hyperlinks is what makes the browser so useful and necessary for searching, viewing, and retrieving information. We will discuss more about the mechanics of Internet browsing in Chapter 4.

Exploring Web Pages

This is a good time to talk a little about Web pages. The word "web" in the context of the Internet comes from the term world-wide-web, or www. The world-wide-web consists of computers that store and connect related documents through interconnected hypertext links. A document on one computer's web page may be linked electronically to a document on the same or different computer. You navigate a Web page by clicking on the hypertext links. Links may be text or graphics.

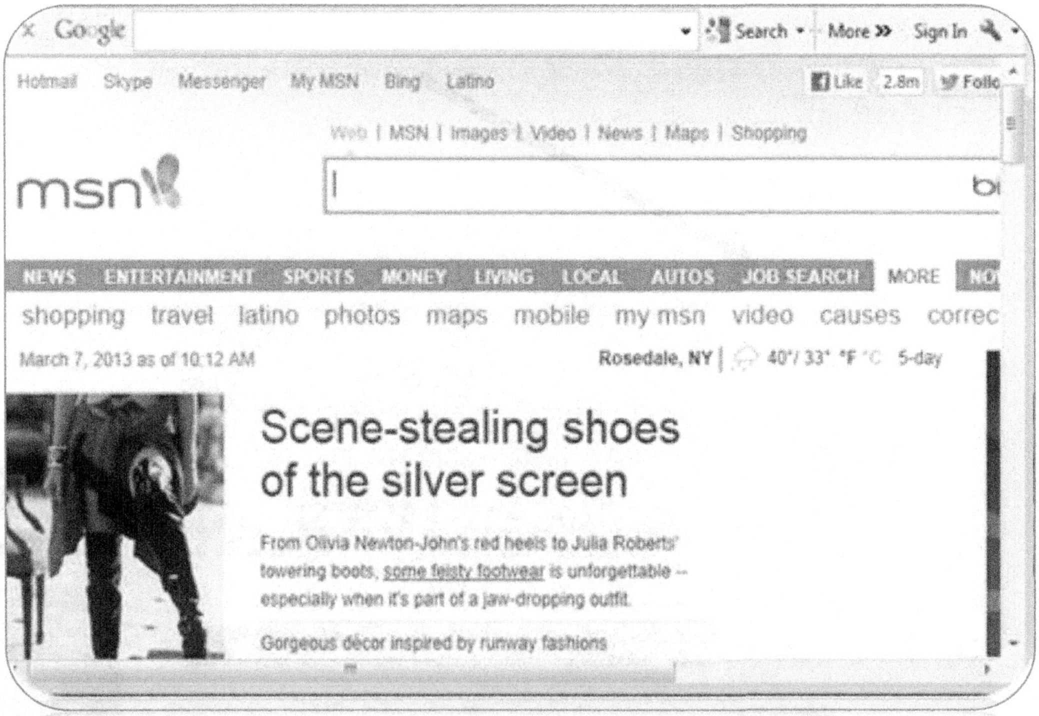

Figure 8

A Web Page from MSN.com

When we click on the Mail link depicted in Figure 9, another page is displayed. This time an advertisement appears. Companies like Google and Yahoo earn income by selling advertising on their Web sites. Notice too, how one must either sign in or create an account to access Yahoo Mail, a free program. The sign in process is a required first level security procedure for every e-mail program. We'll discuss e-mail in greater detail in Chapter 5.

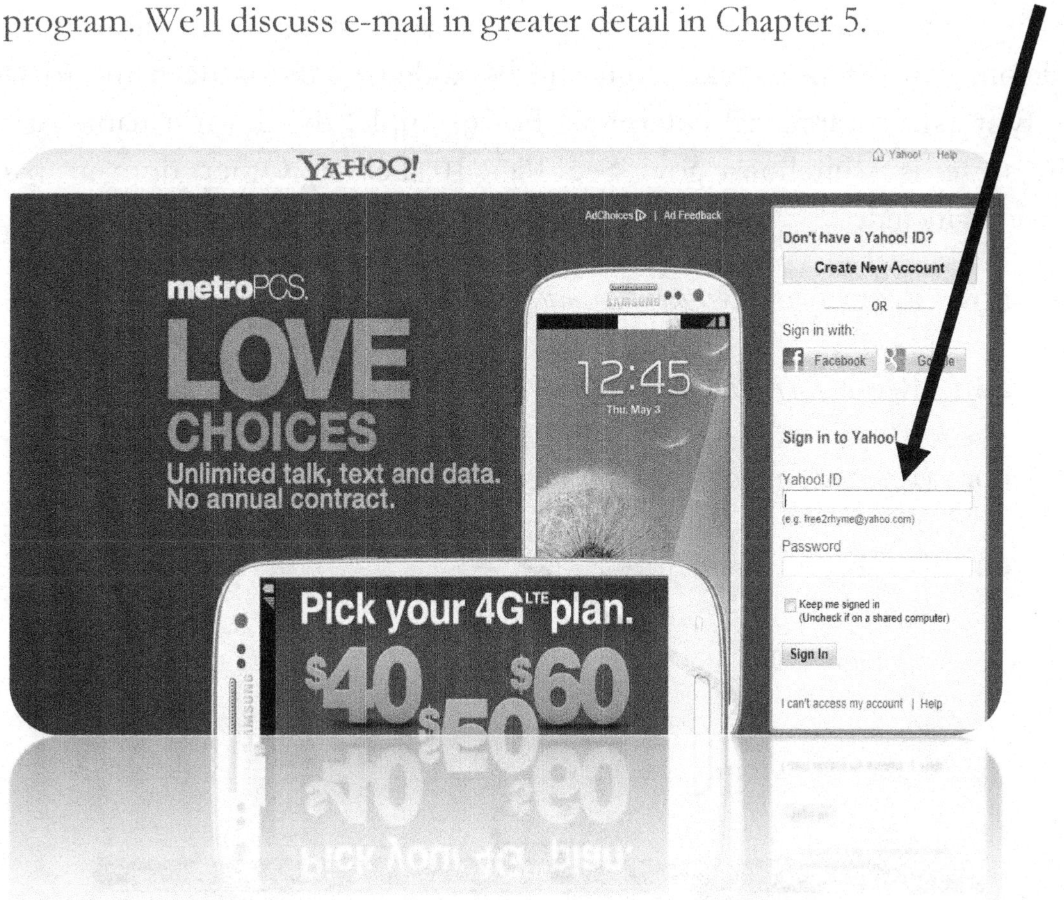

Figure 9

Understanding Domain Names

Every network and computer connected to the Internet is given a unique address. These addresses are largely numeric in format which is great for computers, but isn't as helpful to humans. Because we humans generally find it easier to remember letters, Internet addresses may also be located by entering an easy-to-remember nickname, like Microsoft.com. Think of the domain name as describing the address where a computer network resides. If an organization or individual wishes to have a presence on the Internet, one of the first things they will need to do is to register their domain name with any of the many agencies authorized to distribute these names. To facilitate the identification of a domain, a universal naming convention was developed. Commercial organizations generally want to use their trade names as part of their domain name. Consider such popular domain names as ibm.com, or pepsi.com. An extension like .com will be added to the trade name to help identify it as a commercial enterprise. For example, the domain name of the Whitehouse is whitehouse.gov. See Fig. 10 below. Other domain name extensions include:

- **.gov** *(Reserved for government agencies)*
- **.edu** *(Reserved for educational institutions)*
- **.com** *(Reserved for commercial organizations)*
- **.co** *(Reserved for Countries)*

Figure 10

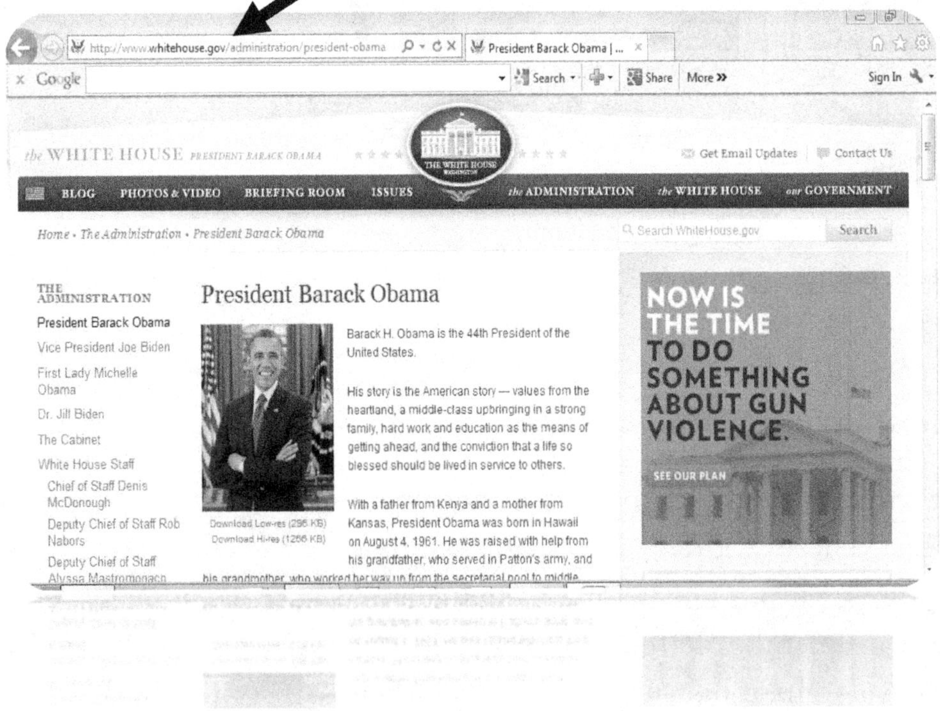

Now that you understand a little about domain names and browsers, you are ready to begin the process of surfing the Web.

Chapter Review Questions

1. List the requirements for establishing an Internet connection *(Hint Pg. 12)*

____

____

____

____

2. Describe what Internet Service Providers offer. *(Hint Pg. 13)*

____

____

____

3. Explain the purpose and function of a browser. *(Hint Pg. 14)*

____

____

____

4. List three domain name extensions *(Hint Pg. 16)*

____

____

____

My Notes:

Chapter 3
Navigating the Web

- Identify Internet Addresses
- Use Search Engines to Find Information
- Navigate a Website
- Download Files to a Computer
- Identify Social Media Sites

Surfing the World Wide Web

Searching for information on the Internet is often referred to as "surfing." Because there are literally thousands of computers connected to the web, containing all kinds of information, it is important that you understand a little something about tools designed to help you find what you are looking for.

Let us suppose that a friend indicates that she purchased a book online (via the Internet). She tells you that you can find the website by launching your browser program and typing in a universal resource locator (URL) such as http://www.amazon.com. Well, you might be thinking what the heck does that mean? Http stands for hypertext transfer protocol. It's the set of communications rules used to connect World Wide Web sites across the Internet.

The standard way to state the address of any resource on the Internet is to type into the browser program, the standard protocol, http:// followed by **www** and then the domain name. See Figure 11 below. When you type this URL, you will arrive at the **Amazon.com** website.

Figure 11

Let us suppose that you are planning to have a few friends over for dinner. You want to cook something special like chicken cordon bleu; however, you don't have a recipe. If you think the chances are pretty good that you will find one on the Internet, then you get a gold star. To find your recipe, you will need to use one of the many search engines available on the Internet. According to the people at Netlingo.com, "A search engine is simply a program that acts as a card catalog of the Internet."[1]

There are several search engines on the Internet, each developed by companies interested in making the Internet easier to use for both consumers and vendors. Examples of Search Engine developers include Google.com, Bing.com, Lycos.com, and Yahoo.com. If you are in front of your computer, launch your browser and then type within the Internet Address field the following: http://www.google.com. Within the Google search field, type chicken cordon bleu. Those are our "search terms." See Figure 12.

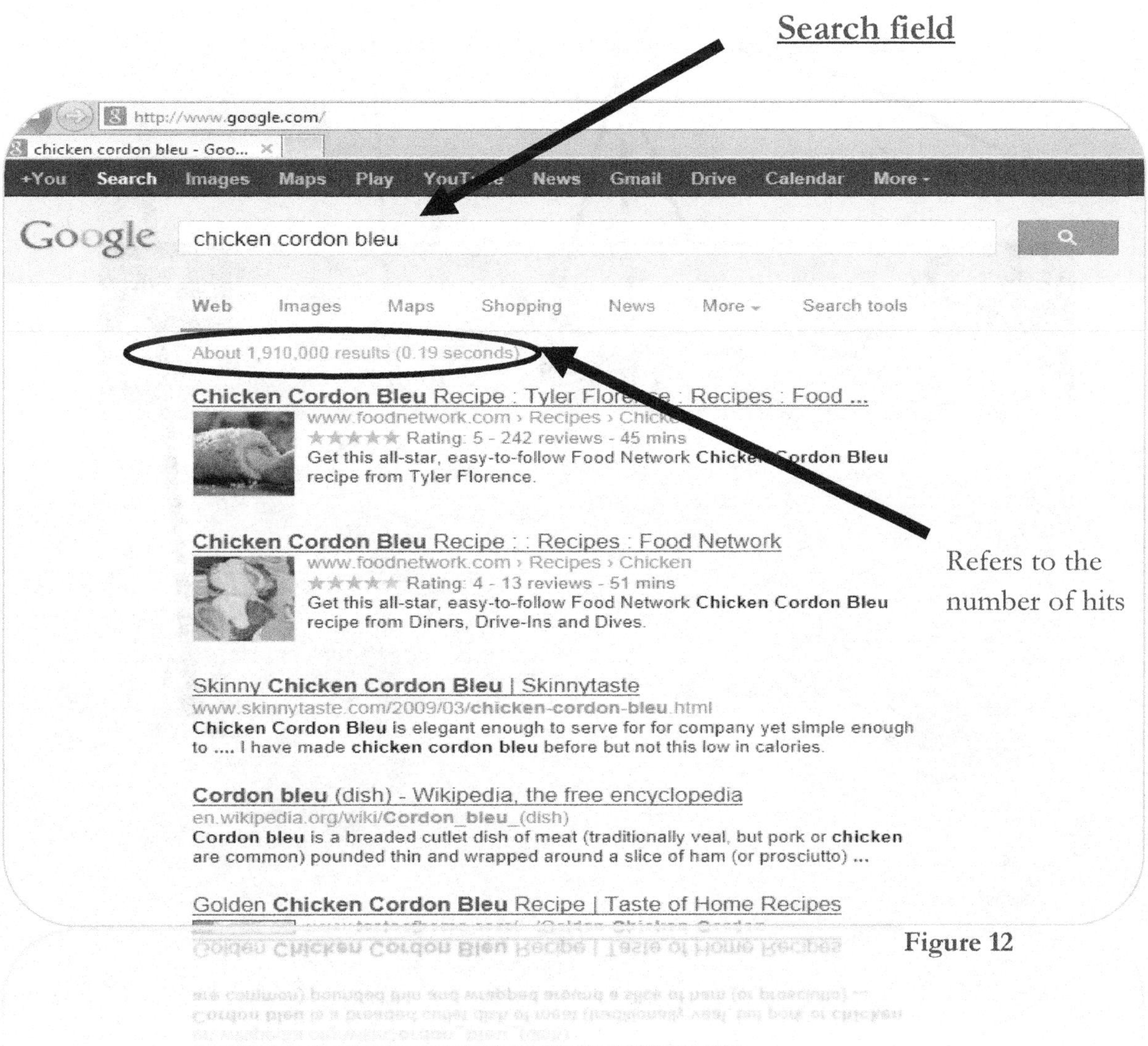

Figure 12

[1] Netlingo. "http://www.netlingo.com/word/search-engine.php." (accessed March 10, 2013).

Google's search engine retrieves more than 1,910,000 results or "hits". No, your eyes are not deceiving you. Nearly 2 million hits are being displayed. To view any one of the search results, you must click on their hyperlinks. Figure 13 below represents the first hit, which is a page from the Food Network Web site. To navigate within this website, all you really need to do is move your mouse around the page to identify links to other pages. Aside from underlined text, a picture may also represent a link. Web sites generally adhere to certain conventions. For example, generally a Web site will have navigation buttons appearing either along the left side of the page or the along the top.

Figure 13

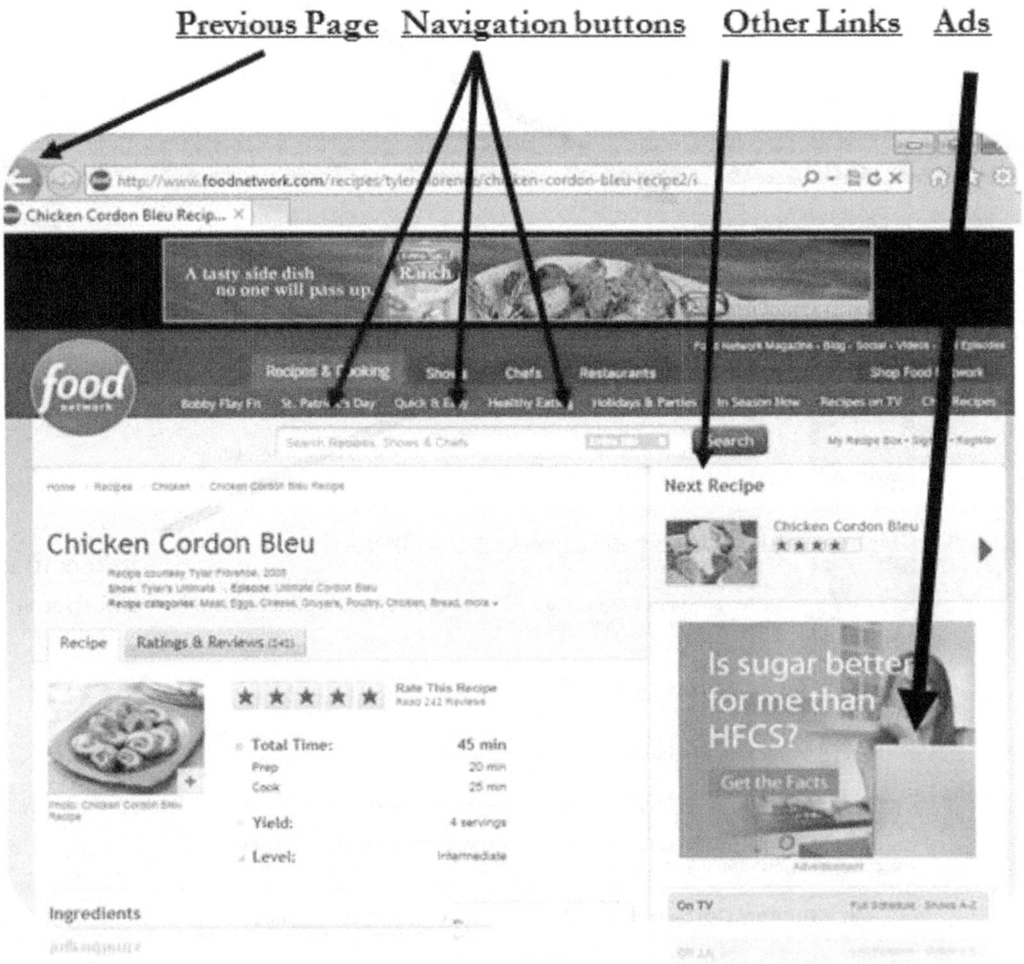

Downloading Files from the Internet

One of the first questions my students always ask me to do is explain what the term "downloading" means. They have heard their children and grandchildren use the term, but they are nevertheless at a loss to explain exactly what it means. The simple fact is that to "download" means to copy data or information from one computer to another. The ability to transfer files is a key feature of the Internet. So what exactly can be downloaded? Almost anything and everything can be downloaded. In other words, music, photographs, documents, recipes, maps, you name it.

Let's take a look at what those crazy kids are doing shall we? Launch your browser and type in the following Internet address: **http://www.apple.com/itunes/**

Figure 14

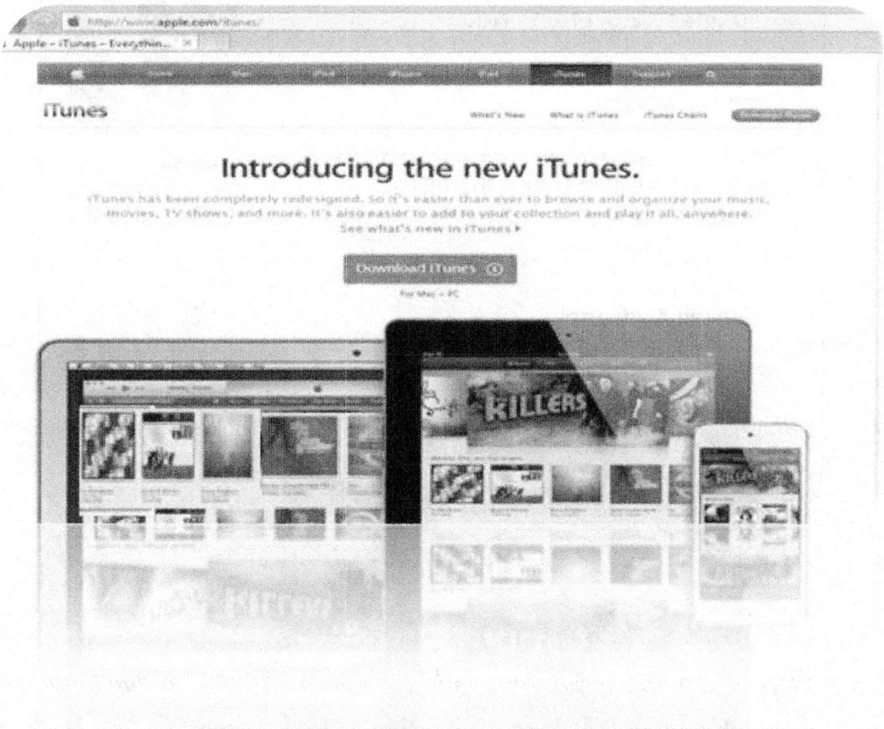

Purchase, download and listen to your favorite rock, jazz, or blues,

Itunes is a product of Apple Computer. After entering into agreements with music companies, Apple is permitted to store recordings in electronic or "digital" form on their fileservers. For a fee, Apple then licenses that music to consumers, who are in-turn, permitted to download or "copy" the songs or albums of their choice to their personal computers.

Once the free Itunes program has been downloaded to your computer you will be able to purchase, copy and listen to that music on your computer, IPod, or perhaps even your cell phone.

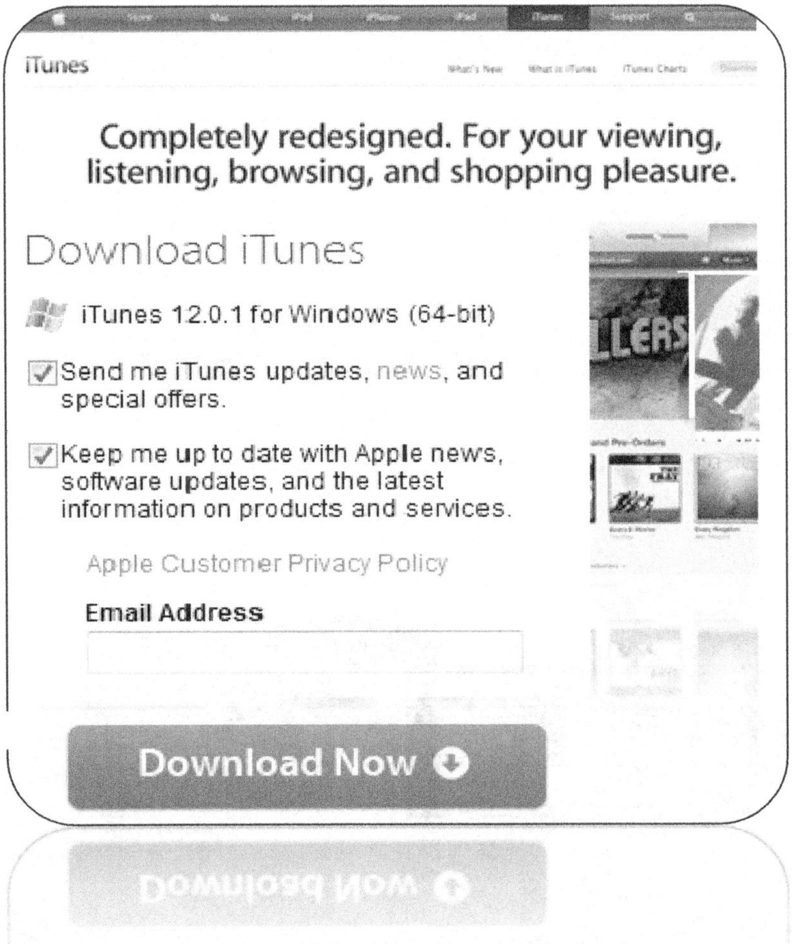

Figure 15

Please keep in mind that you only hold a revocable license to download music you have purchased online. It is a violation of U.S. copyright law to share or redistribute that music without permission.

More About Downloading

There is of course more to the Internet than just downloading music. For example, suppose you come across an interesting Web site containing a great recipe for macaroni and cheese. You have a number of options. You can print out a copy of the Web page, you can memorize the content of the Web page, you can take notes, or, in many cases you can simply transfer the information to your computer. And as I mentioned, you may also want to transfer that data to your cell phone as well. Let's examine Figure 16 below. Notice the convenient links for printing, emailing, and sending to a mobile device.

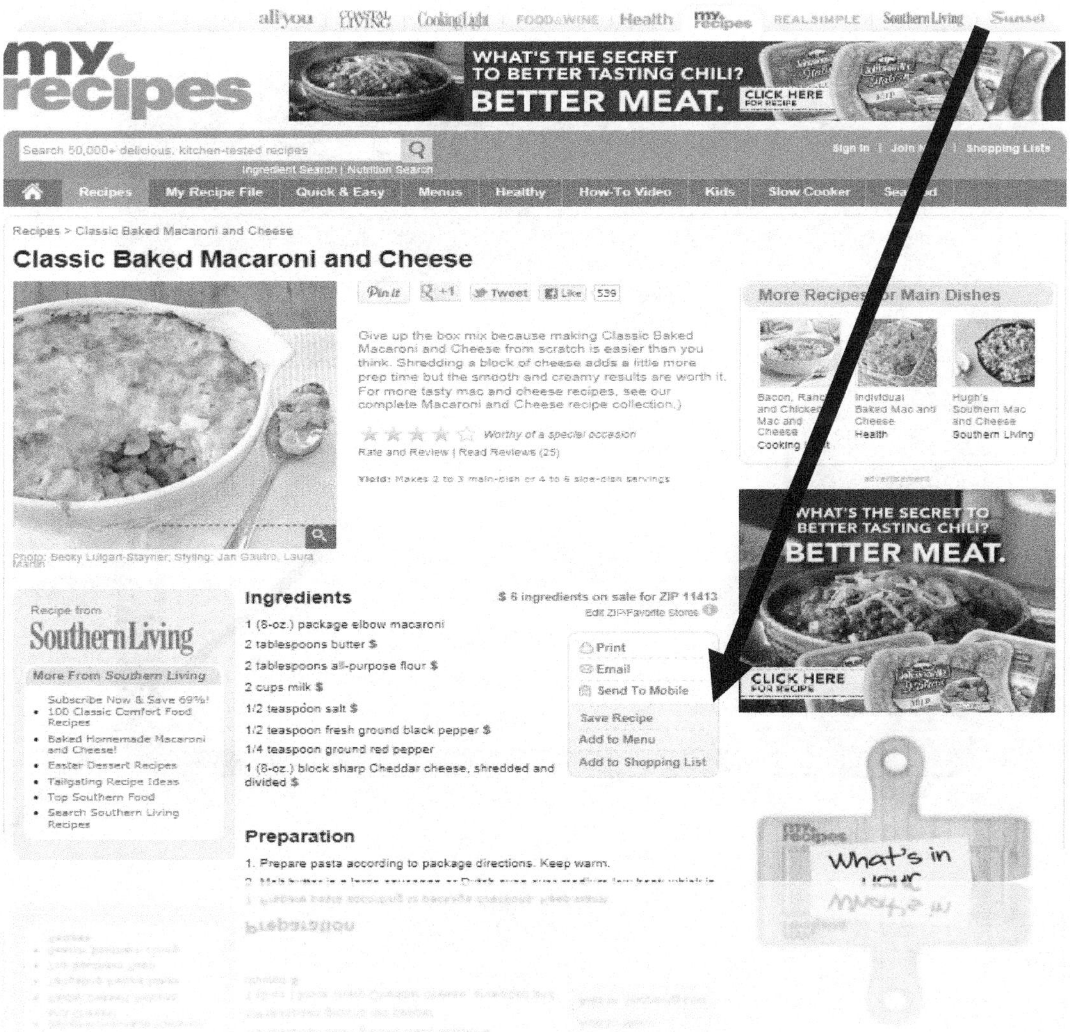

Figure 16

We found this tasty recipe at http://www.myrecipes.com.

Downloading to a Mobile Device

Browser programs like Internet Explorer or Safari enable you to view information on the Internet. Search engines in contrast are somewhat like card catalogs, in that they are designed to index and retrieve information that matches your search terms. Popular search engines include Google, Yahoo, Bing and Lycos.

To summarize, you have learned that a major advantage of the Internet is found in the ability we have to quickly search and download all kinds' information to our computers and other electronic devices.

Figure 17

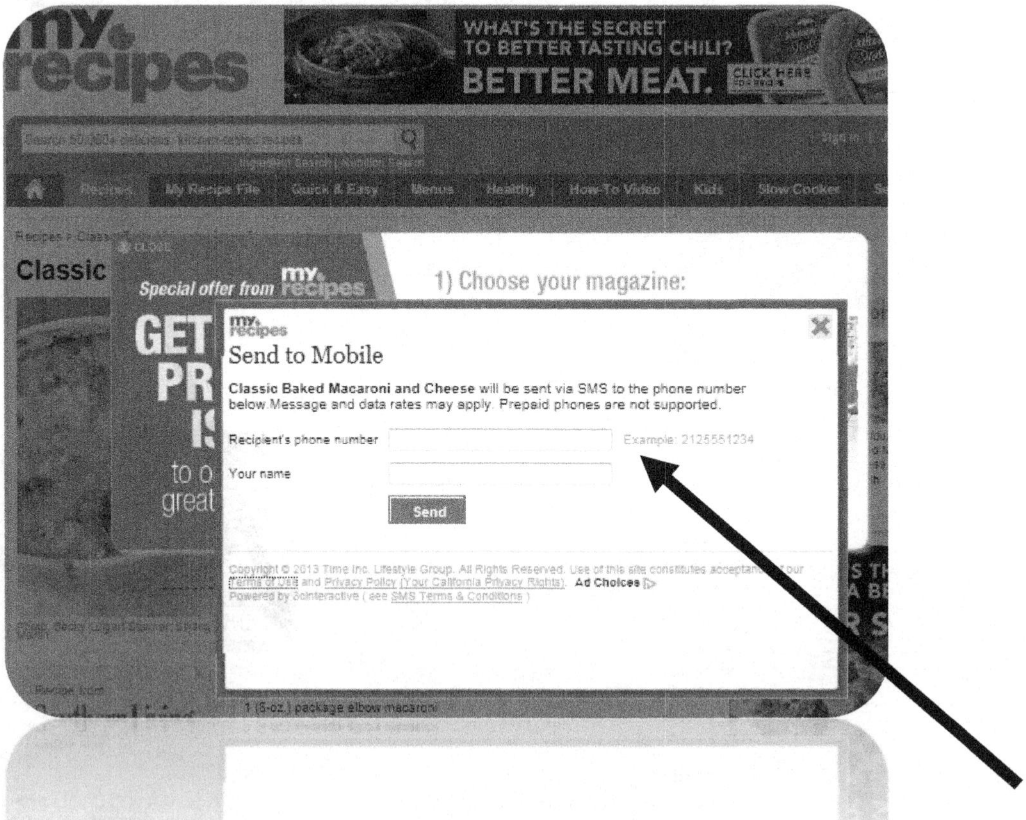

Connecting with Others through Social Media

One of the most popular applications of the Internet today is collectively referred to as social media. As you have no doubt learned by now, through the Internet it is possible to communicate with others who are also connected to the Web. You have probably heard friends or family members talking about Facebook, Myspace, Twitter, and LinkedIn. For example, if your granddaughter wants to put pictures on Facebook or post information about a day in her life, what she is really talking about is using a social media website that provides her with the ability to share this information with others. LinkedIn on the other hand, is targeted to business professionals.

Signing-up to join one of the many social media sites requires that you set-up an account, by creating a username and password. Once you do that, you get to create a little personal Web page and profile, where you can post all kinds of information, including the family album. For instance, my friend Michele can share her trip to Europe, and let all of her friends post messages about them. See the pretend page in Figure 18 below. She might also be able to write a "blog" about travel in general. What's a blog? Well you might think of a blog as an electronic journal where you can share your thoughts and ideas with others, and they in turn can respond.

Instant messaging is another feature you may encounter on social networking sites, and increasingly on business sites. This feature enables you to send quick messages and share images with others who are also part of the same network.

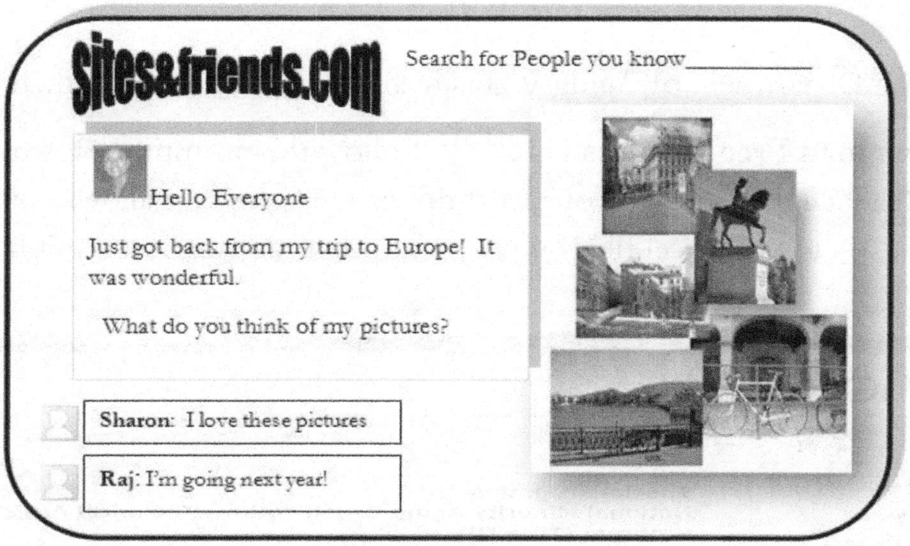

Figure 18

Elements of a Social Media Page

Chapter Review Questions

1. Launch Internet Explorer and then type into the address bar the following Internet address: **www.disney.com**

2. Locate and click on the some of the links on this Web page.

3. Are any of the links pictures? **Yes** **No**

4. List at least three (3) links that appear on the page.

- ______________________________
- ______________________________
- ______________________________

5. In the address bar, type the following Internet address**: www.google.com**

6. Type the words Internet dictionary into the Google search field.

7. How many search results did the Google search engine retrieve? _______

8. Go to the Department of Aging Web site at **www.aoa.gov**, and then click on the **Download Free Readers** link.  Follow the prompt to download the Excel Reader application to your hard-drive. This program allows you to open and view Microsoft Excel files on your computer, even if you don't have Excel.

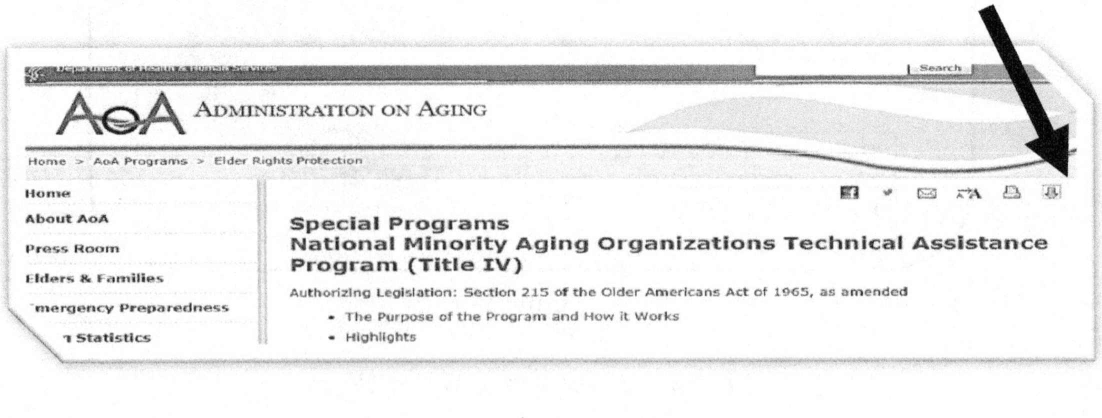

My Notes:

My Notes:

Chapter 4

Working with Internet Explorer Browser Controls

- Use Internet Explorer's Favorites Feature
- Use Zoom to Control Magnification
- Print a Web Page
- Save a Web Page

Getting Familiar with the Internet Explorer Environment

It's a good idea to become a little more familiar with the Internet Explorer, (IE) environment, since you will likely be using IE on a fairly regular basis. Take a few minutes to review these screen elements before moving on to such features as the Tools button and the Favorites folder.

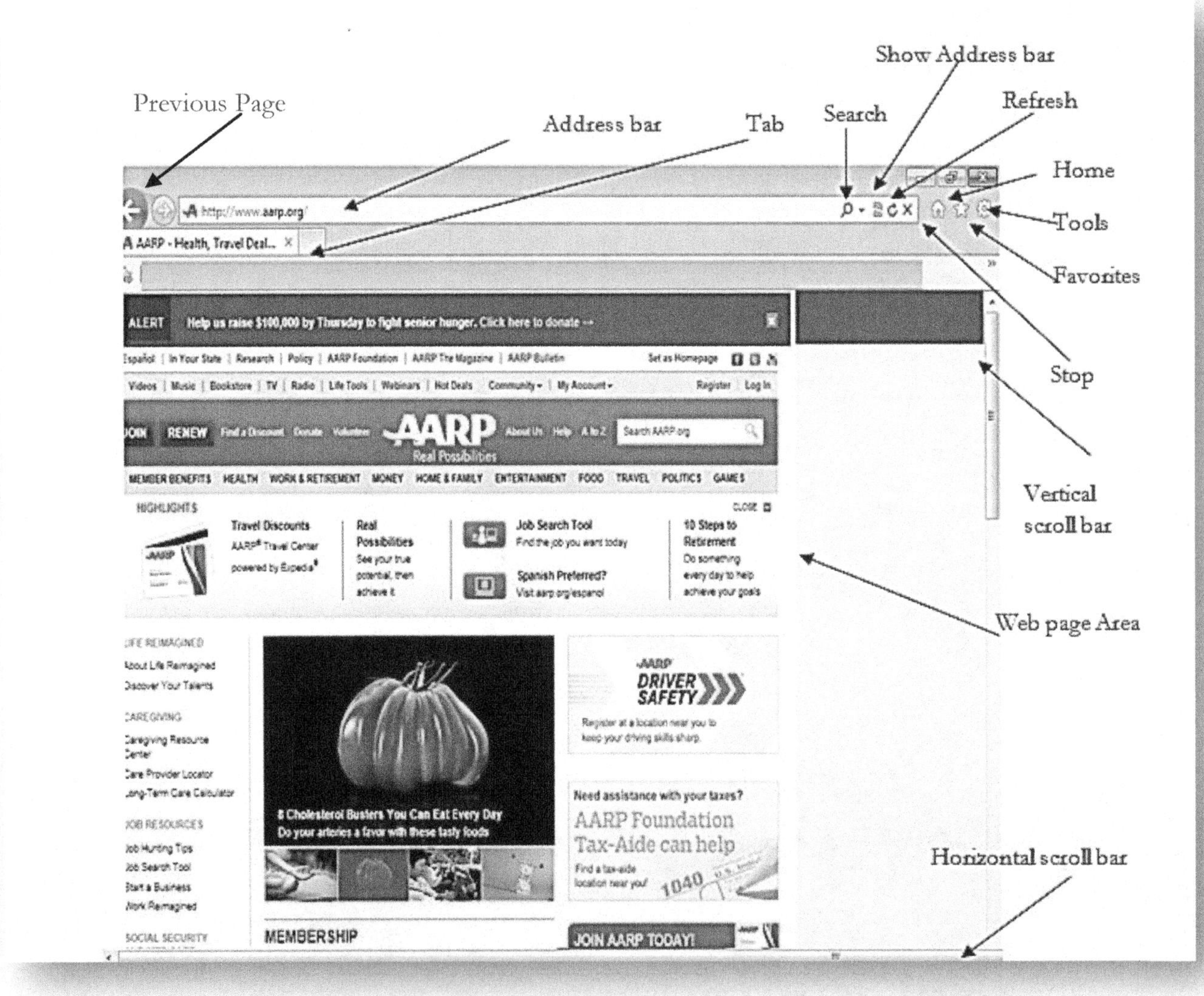

Figure 19

Practice moving both the horizontal and vertical scroll bars. If you are relatively inexperienced with using a mouse, this is something you will want to get better at doing, since Web pages often require that you scroll up and down to view the content of an entire page.

Internet Explorer Navigation Buttons

Address Bar	Shows the address of the Web page you are viewing. This is also the place you will enter the address of a Web page you wish to visit.
Previous Page:	Clicking on this button takes you to the Web Page you were visiting previously.
Home	The Web page displayed each time you open Internet Explorer
Tools	The button that controls such commands as printing, Print Preview, Save, Zoom Control, Safety and Internet Options
Favorites	Allows you to save the addresses of your favorite Web addresses for future use.
Vertical Scroll Bar	Moves the page in an up or down direction. Use this when you can't see everything on the screen.
Horizontal Scroll Bar	Moves the page from side to side.
Tab	Displays the name of the Web site you are visiting.
New Tab	Opens a new tab to facilitate searching a new Web site.
Search	Click on this button to view and select previously visited sites.
Refresh	Refreshes the screen- useful when a page fails to load or display properly.
Stop	Stops displaying or searching for the URL entered into the Address bar.
Web Page Area:	The area is where your Web page content is displayed.

Book Marks and Favorites

While surfing the Internet, you will no doubt, come across Web sites that you will want to revisit. Over time, it can be difficult to remember a given Internet address. Like most browsers, Microsoft's Internet Explorer makes it possible to "bookmark" a favorite site. For example, suppose you have visited the medicare.gov Web site and wish to bookmark it. All you have to do is save it to the Favorites folder using the Internet Explorer's Tools menu located in the top right corner.

To save the medicare.gov Web site, we need to click on the "star" icon, and then click on the Add to Favorites Button.

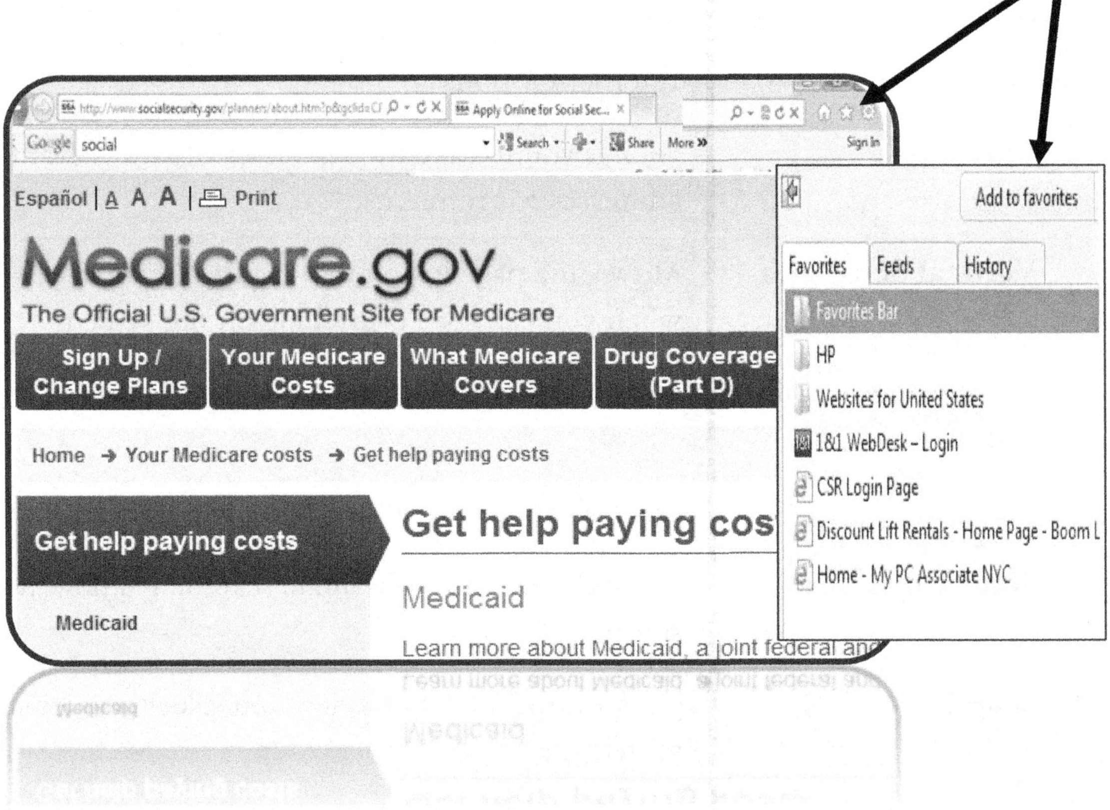

Figure 20

The Web pages you save to your Favorites folder will save you the time of having to type in an Internet address each time you go online. The Favorites bar is displayed as open in Figure 20.

Using Zoom Control

If you are a baby-boomer like me, you might appreciate Internet Explorer's zoom control feature. This is a wonderful option, as it permits you to control the magnification of text on the screen. You can access the magnification option by clicking on the Tools button. You will find the Tools button located to the right of the Favorites button. The Tools button looks like a little gear. See Figure 21.

Figure 21

Click on the Zoom menu option to adjust the magnification of text on the screen. These settings can be changed at any time from Web site to Web site.

Note that the zoom control options will not alter how large the text will be if you decide to print the Web page.

Printing on the Web

When you find useful information on the Web, you will likely want a hard copy of that information. For this reason, having a reliable printer attached to your computer will be a necessity. Fortunately, printing on the Internet is a fairly simple task. Once again, if you are working with Internet Explorer, you will need to perform the following steps:

1. Click on the Tools button
2. Click on the Print menu option
3. When your printer's dialog box opens, click on the Print button

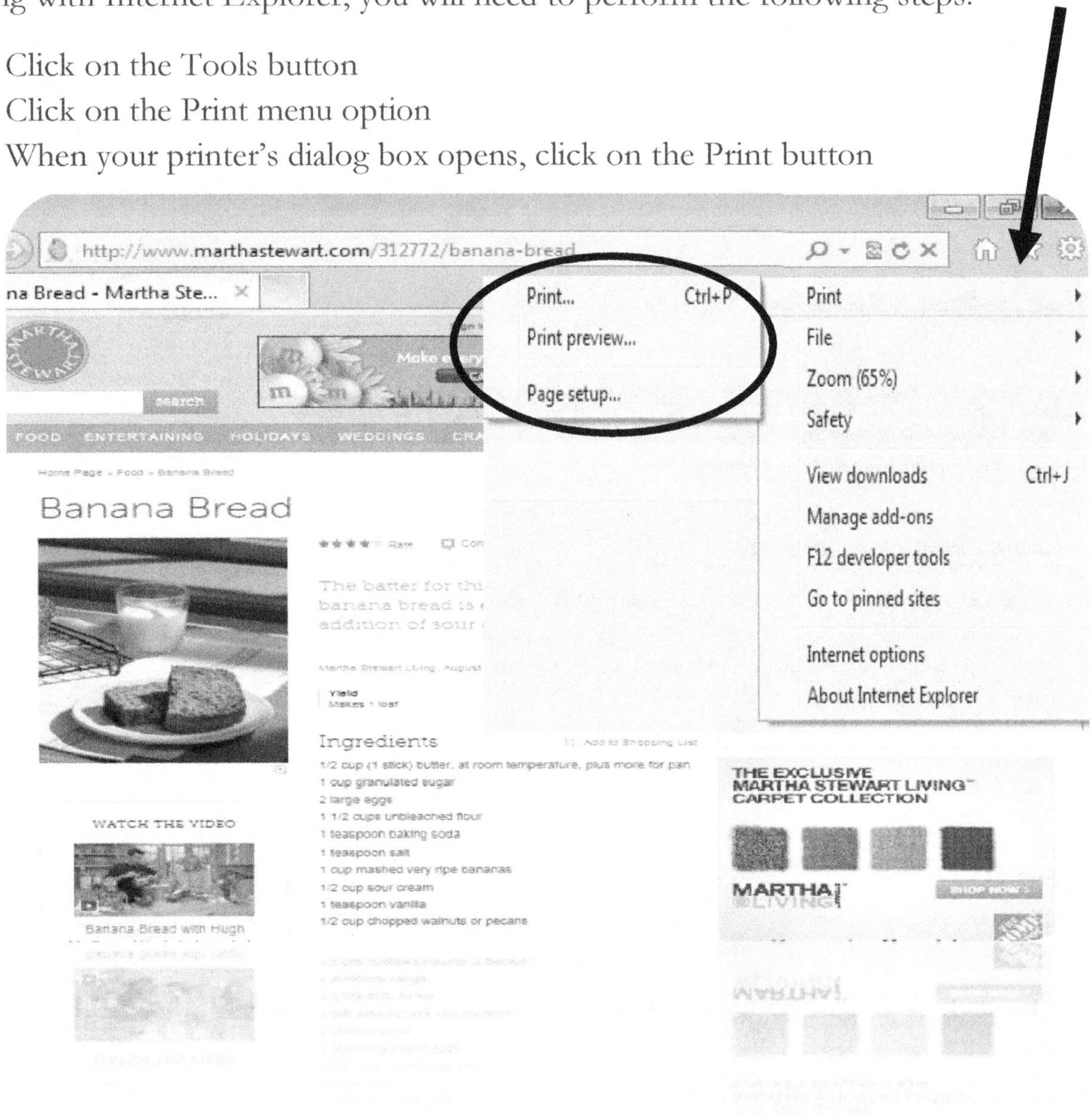

Figure 22

If you want to see a preview of what your Web page will look like when printed, choose the Print preview option. In addition, if you want to change page orientation say from the default portrait style to landscape, you will need to choose the page setup menu option.

Saving a Web Page or Document

Many organizations engage in public relations or public service by providing resources to visitors of their Web sites. Everything from government documents and applications to recipes are available. Until now, you have learned how to view, print, and bookmark a Web page. However, you will find it useful to be able to save a Web Page to your computer's hard drive for future reference. With Internet Explorer, this is a fairly straightforward task. To print a Web page, perform the following steps:

1. Click on the Tools button
2. Select the File menu option
3. Choose the Save as menu option
4. Click on the Save button

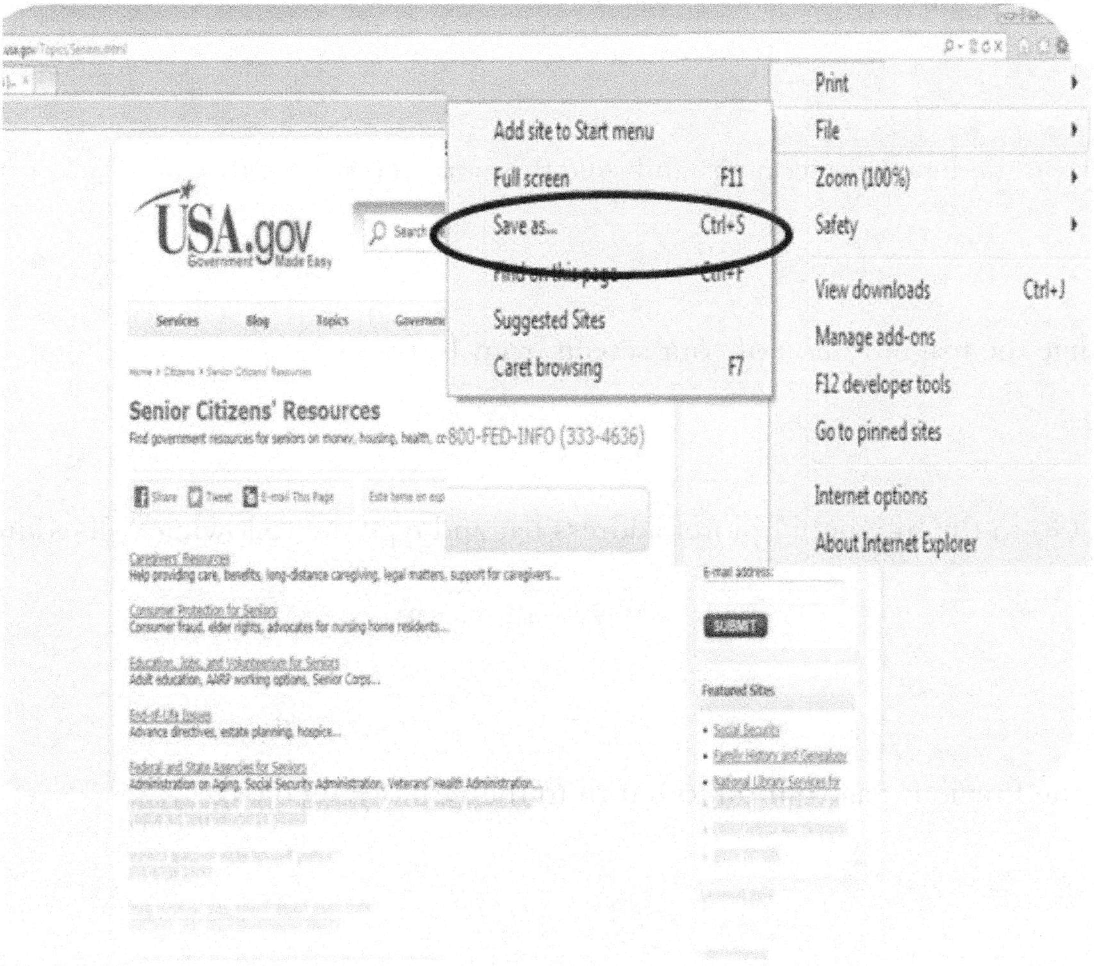

Figure 23

The Save as menu option saves a copy of the desired Web page to your hard-drive.

Chapter Review Questions

1. Go to the Internet Explorer address bar and type the following Web address:

   www.aarp.org

2. Using the Tools button, print a copy of the Web page.

3. Save the Web page as AARP Web page.

4. Click on the Favorites icon ★ and save the aarp web page into your Favorites folder.

5. Change the magnification of your screen from 100% to 75%.

6. Go to the Internet Explorer address bar and type the following Web address:

   www.yahoo.com

7. Use the Previous page button to return to the aarp.org Web page.

My Notes:

My Notes:

Chapter 5

E-Mail with Microsoft's Outlook.com

- Register for an Outlook.com E-mail Account
- Sign-in to the Outlook.com Application
- Compose an E-Mail Message
- Reply to an E-Mail Message
- Print E-Mail Messages

E-Mail and Why You Need It

As we have discussed, one of the advantages of networking computers is the ability to share and communicate information seamlessly. Remember, connecting or networking computers makes e-mail possible. E-mail, the electronic transmission of messages is so important in today's society. When nearly every business and government agency communicates electronically, it becomes important that you be connected as well. In this chapter, we will introduce you to the process of creating an e-mail account. You will also learn how to compose, send, reply to and manage e-mail messages.

Setting-Up an E-Mail Account

I have good news for you. In less than about 10 minutes, you can create an e-mail account, and start communicating with everyone you know at no cost to you. Why? Well, this is largely because e-mail providers earn revenue by monetizing their websites. Put simply, these e-mail providers allow third parties to advertise and market goods on their websites to e-mail users. Those revenues earned by the e-mail provider support the costs of making e-mail available for free.

When you sign-up for one of these free e-mail services, you will nevertheless have to create an account so you can become part of that provider's e-mail network. However, as a security precaution each e-mail program requires that you open an account. In effect, you will be required to submit such information as your name, telephone number, date of birth, etc. We will introduce you to e-mail using Microsoft's Outlook.Com program; however, there are other e-mail programs. In the U.S., companies such as America Online, Comcast, Google, Verizon, and Yahoo offer Internet users e-mail access. You may even find yourself setting up and maintaining more than one e-mail account- That's just fine. Many people have e-mail accounts with an employer, yet maintain multiple personal accounts.

Creating an Outlook.com E-mail Account

To begin the process of setting up an account you will need to perform the following steps:

1. Go to the Outlook.com Web site. www.outlook.com
2. Click on the Try Outlook.com link.

At this point you will see an account form. Carefully complete the form as depicted on your screen. Before you create your account, you may want to familiarize yourself with the form reproduced in part in Figure 25 below.

Figure 25

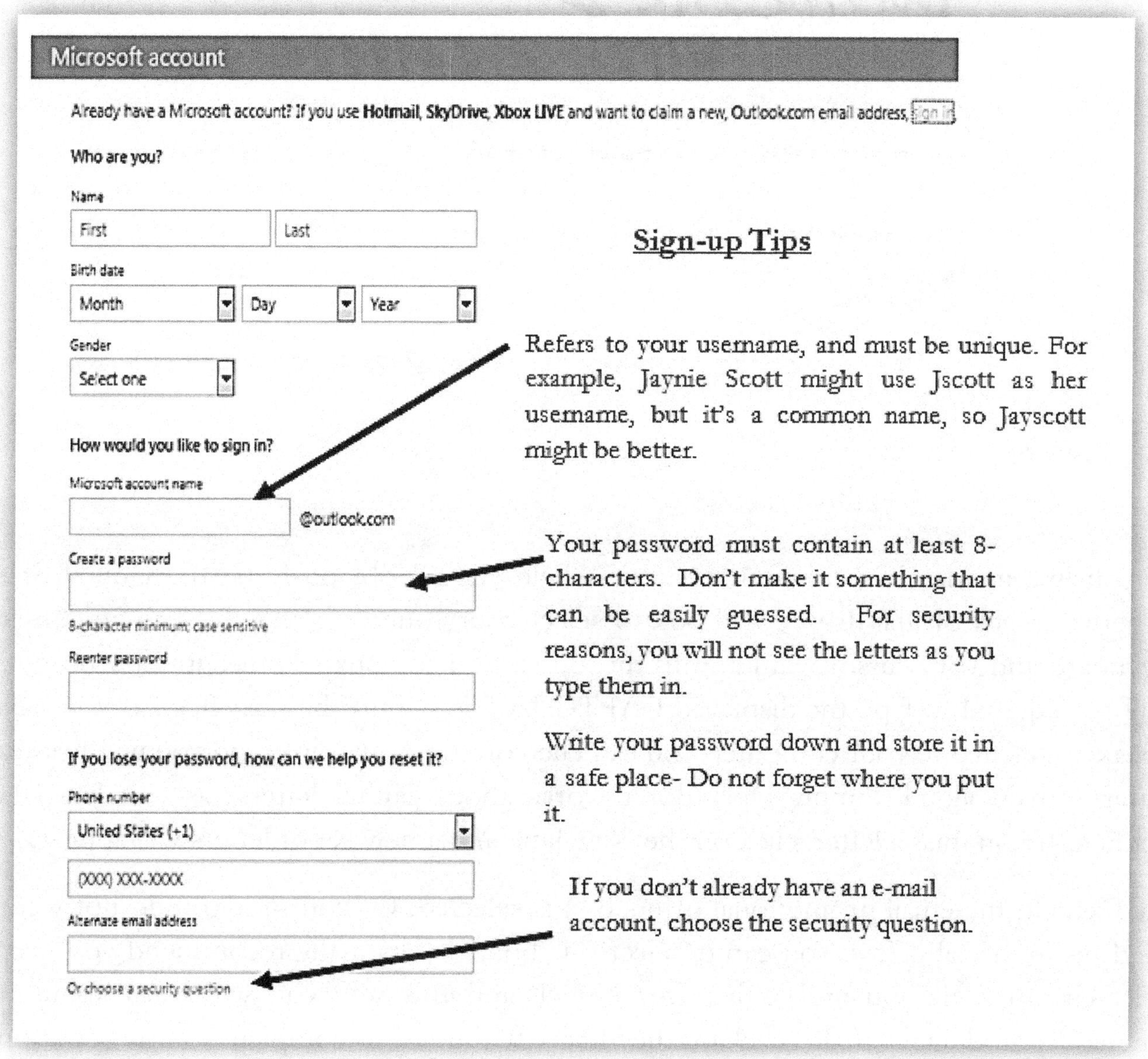

The Second Part of the Form

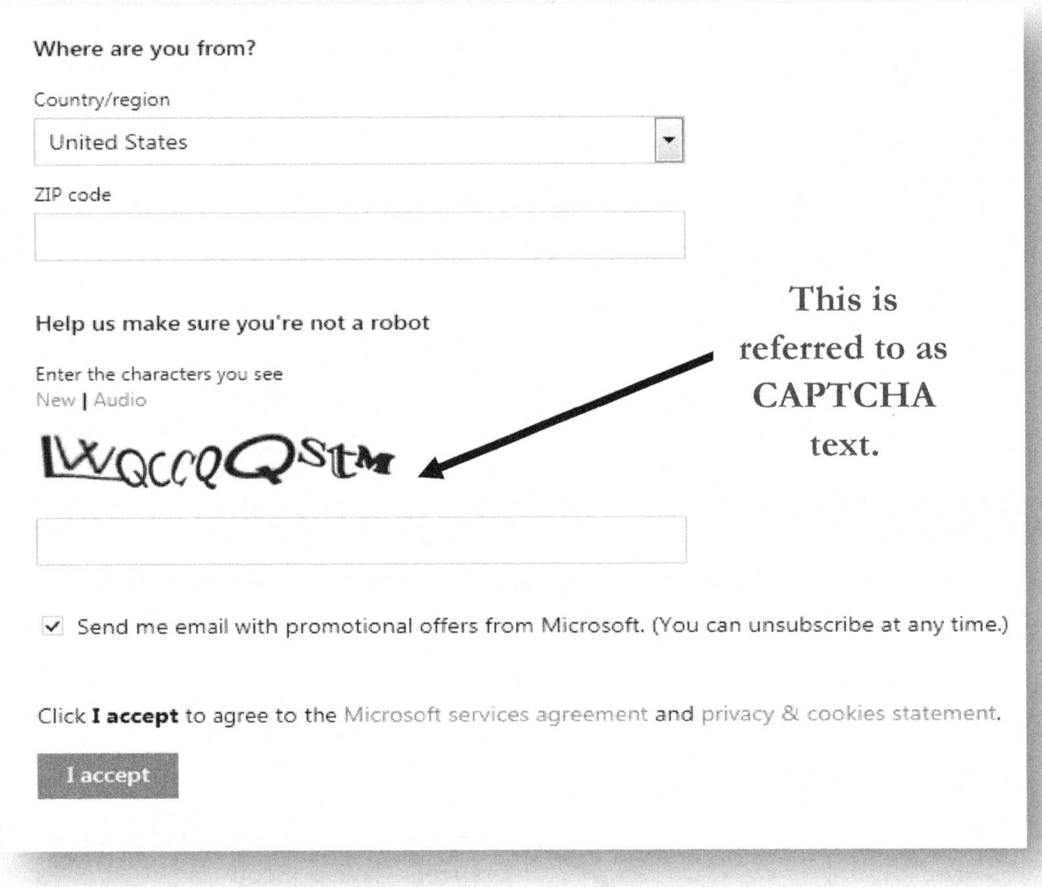

Figure 26

If you live in the U.S., the country/region field should obviously be the United States, otherwise click on the drop down box to select your country. Press the Tab key on your keyboard and your cursor will jump to the zip code field. Next, for security purposes you will be required to type the displayed CAPTCHA letters into the next field. If you have a speaker attached to your computer, you can click on the Audio link, and you will hear each letter spoken aloud. Simply type (don't worry about capital letters) as you hear them spoken. If you miss a letter, click on the New link, and a new set of letters will appear.

By Default, the email promotional offers box is selected. Of course if you do not want to read promotional offers, you can deselect this box. I personally recommend you keep it selected, after all, you are getting free e-mail, and this way you will learn about new Microsoft products. Finally, click on the "I accept" button to complete your registration.

Signing-In to Your Outlook E-Mail Account

After you have completed the Outlook registration process, you will be required to sign-in to your e-mail account using the password and username that you created. Remember, that your username and password are required to ensure that only you, the true owner of the e-mail account gains access to your e-mail account. Take a look at Figure 27. Your screen should resemble the sign-in box depicted here.

Figure 27

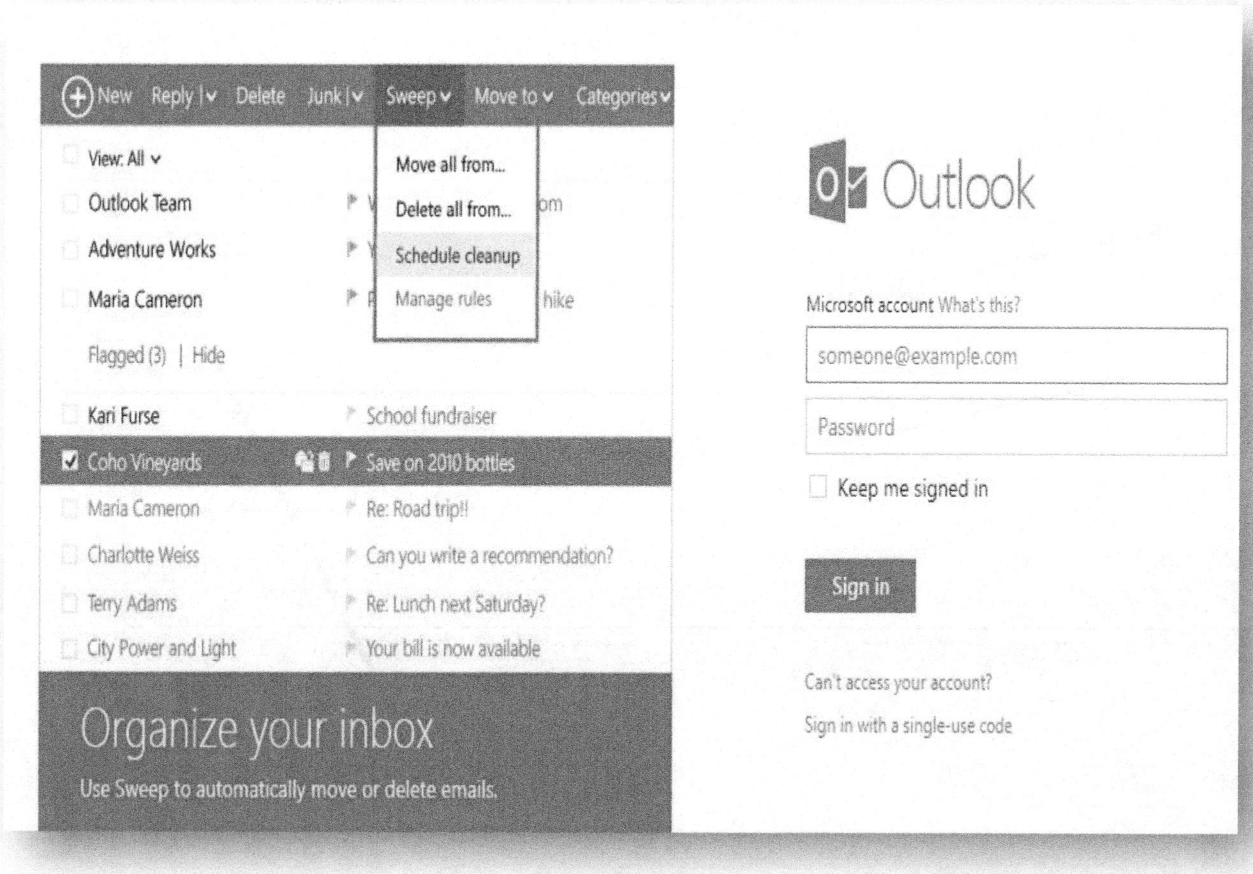

Signing-in to your e-mail account requires that you enter both a username and password.

The Microsoft Outlook.com Environment

After you successfully sign-in to your e-mail account, your e-mail inbox is displayed. As a first-time user of Outlook.com, you will have one new e-mail message from the Outlook team. Examine Figure 28 below.

Figure 28

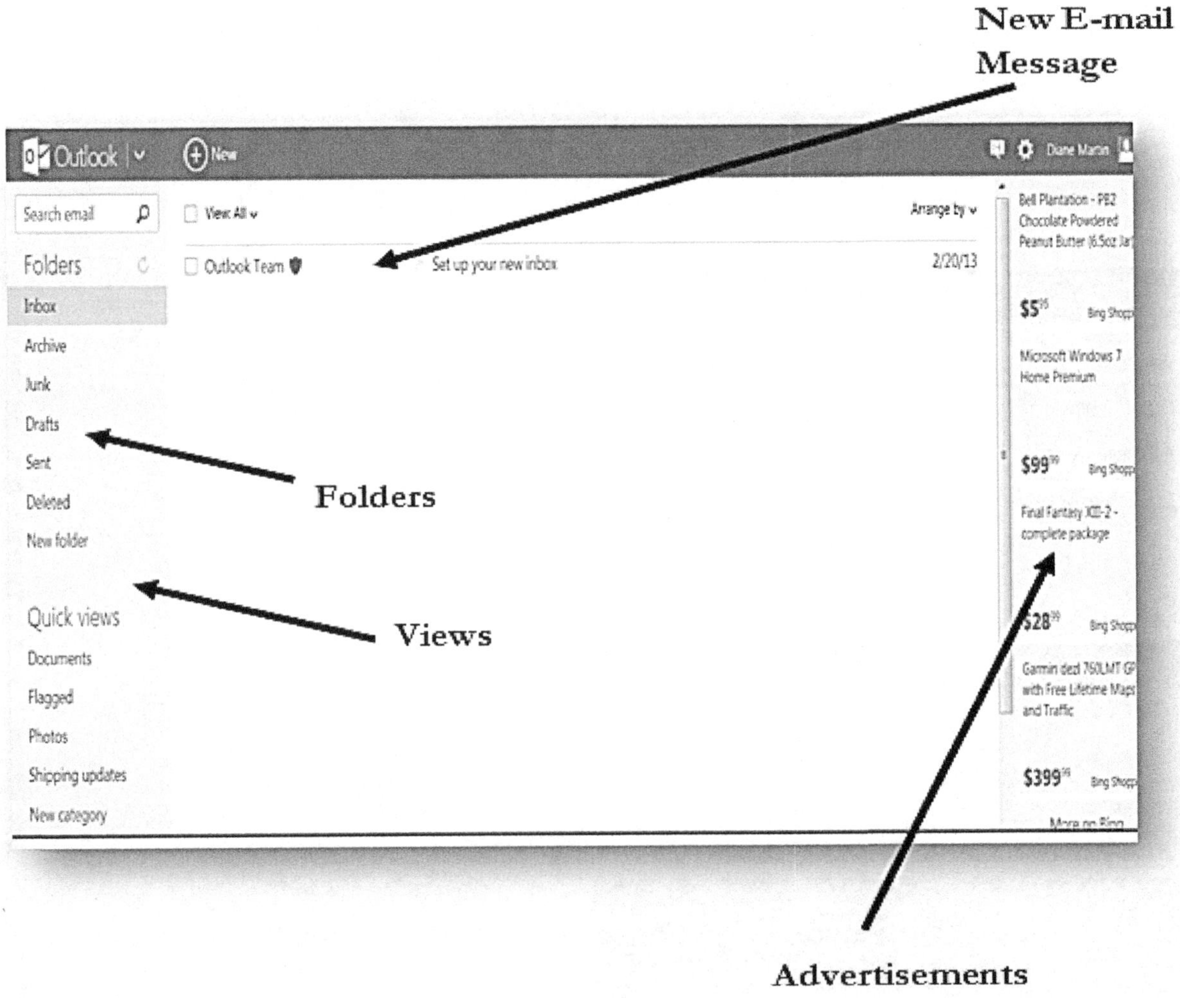

The Outlook.com window consists of a toolbar, inbox (message area) folders, and views. On page 54 you will find a description of each of the default folders and views. With all of the options Outlook offers, you should have no difficulty organizing your e-mail messages. Notice too, that advertisements appear in the navigation bar on the right side of the screen. If you find them annoying, you may upgrade your account to receive what is referred to as ad free e-mail. If you go to the Tools menu, choose More mail settings. There you will find the link for ad free Outlook.

My Notes:

My Notes:

Chapter 6

Viewing and Managing E-Mail

- Open and View E-Mail Messages
- Compose and Send Messages
- Attach a File to an E-Mail Message
- View and Organize Mail by Content
- Print and Save Messages

Opening, Viewing, and Managing E-Mail

When new mail arrives, it is deposited into your inbox. As we discussed, after you create your Outlook e-mail account, a new welcome message will appear in your inbox. See Figure 29 below.

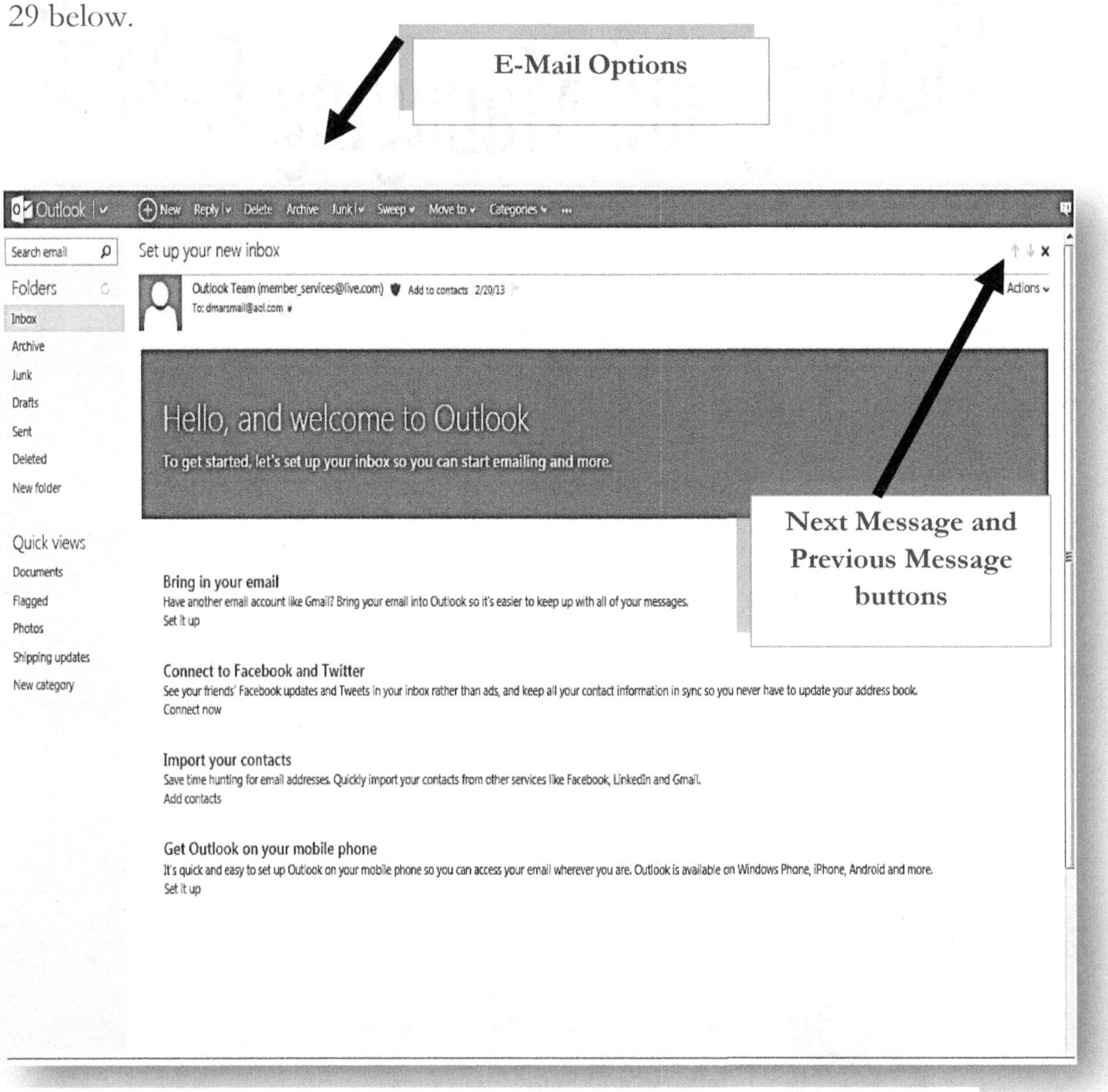

Figure 29

When you open your e-mail, Outlook displays the name and e-mail address of the sender, as well as the date of the message. After reading your e-mail, you have several options. You can continue to read other messages in your inbox by clicking on the Next Message button, located at the top right side of the screen. Alternatively, you can delete the message by clicking on the Delete button located on the toolbar. You also have the option of forwarding the message or replying to the sender.

Composing a New Mail Message

Composing a new mail message with Outlook.com is easy to do. Located on the Toolbar is the New button. Clicking on the New button will cause Outlook to display a screen resembling the one depicted in Figure 30 below.

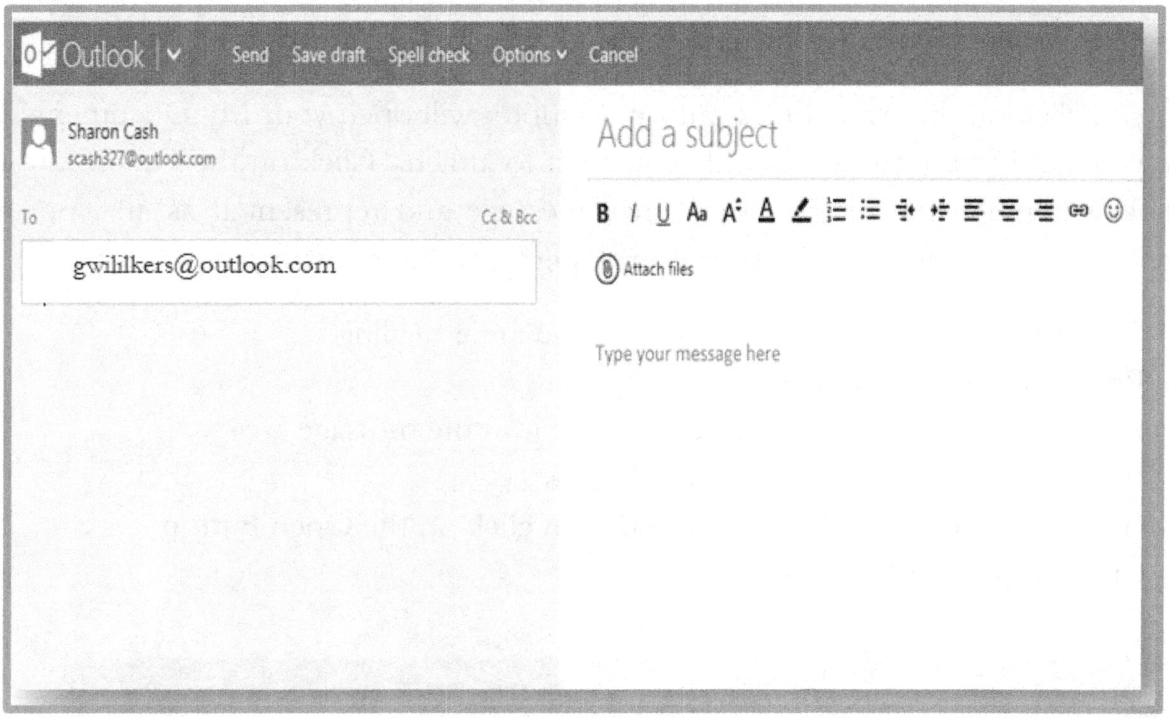

Figure 30

First you will need to address your e-mail message. To do this click your mouse in the To field, then press the Tab key. Pressing the Tab key will cause your cursor to jump to the Add a subject field. Here you can type the subject of your message. Press the Tab key again and your cursor will jump to the message field. After you finish typing your message, simply click on the Send button located on the Outlook Toolbar. See Figure 30 above.

Notice that just above the message field, Outlook displays a button bar. These buttons will enable you to apply character formatting to the text of your e-mail, such as bold, underlining, color, bullets, numbering and spacing. If you want to add a little whimsy to your e-mail, try experimenting with emoticons. These are tiny icons used to facilitate communication. Common emoticons include our little smiley face here. 

Outlook.com also provides a spell checking feature; it is located on the toolbar. It's a good idea to check the spelling of your e-mail message before you send them.

Attaching a File to an E-Mail Message

One of the features you are likely to appreciate about e-mail is the ability to send and receive files. All kinds of files may be "attached" to your e-mail messages, including pictures, documents, presentations, spreadsheets, etc. Any file you have saved to your hard drive may be attached to your e-mail message. All you need to do is type your e-mail message, and then choose the Attach button. See Figure 31 below.

When you click on the Attach files button, Outlook will open your My Documents folder, where you can browse to find the file you wish to attach. Click on the Open button, and Outlook will attach the file to your e-mail message and represent it as an icon in your message area. To attach a file to your e-mail, perform the following steps:

1. Type the e-mail address of the person you are e-mailing.
2. Press the Tab key and then type a subject
3. Press the Tab key and type your message into the message area
4. Click on the Attach files button 

5. Browse to locate the desired file and then click on the Open button
6. Click on the Send button

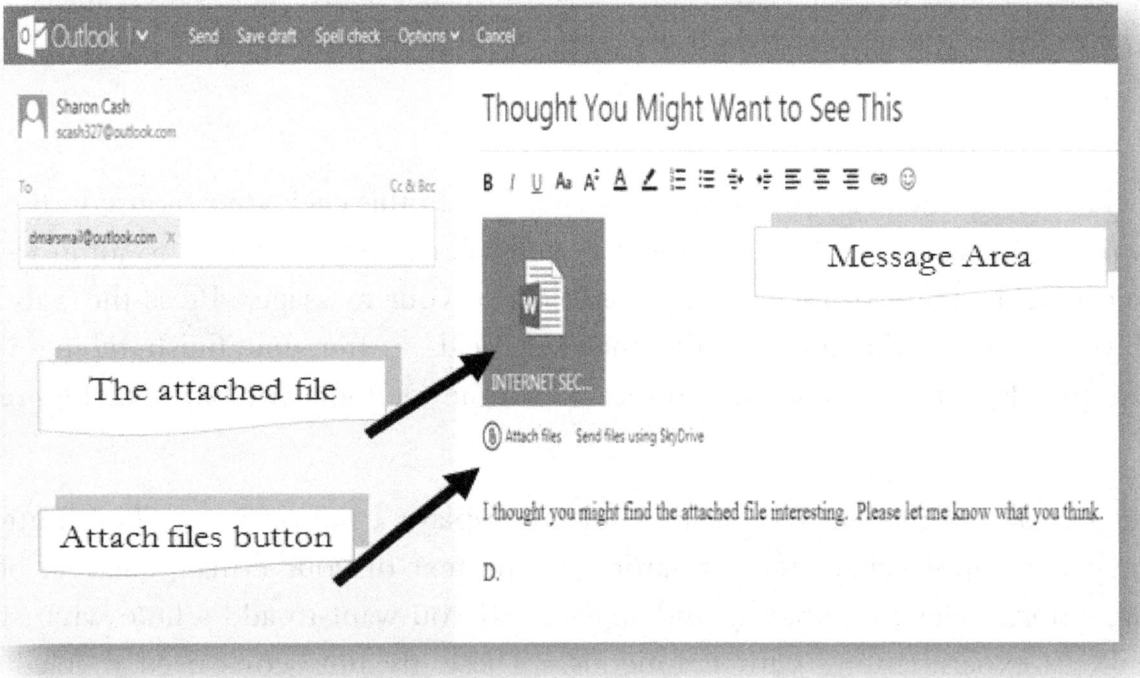

Figure 31

Viewing Messages with Special Content

What makes the Internet and E-mail such a wonderful combination is the ability it gives us to send messages containing different kinds of media, such as documents, music, presentations, and photographs. Outlook enables you to view these types of messages. It also enables you to organize your messages based on their content. For example, examine Figure 32 below and notice the e-mail recipient has received an e-mail containing a photograph.

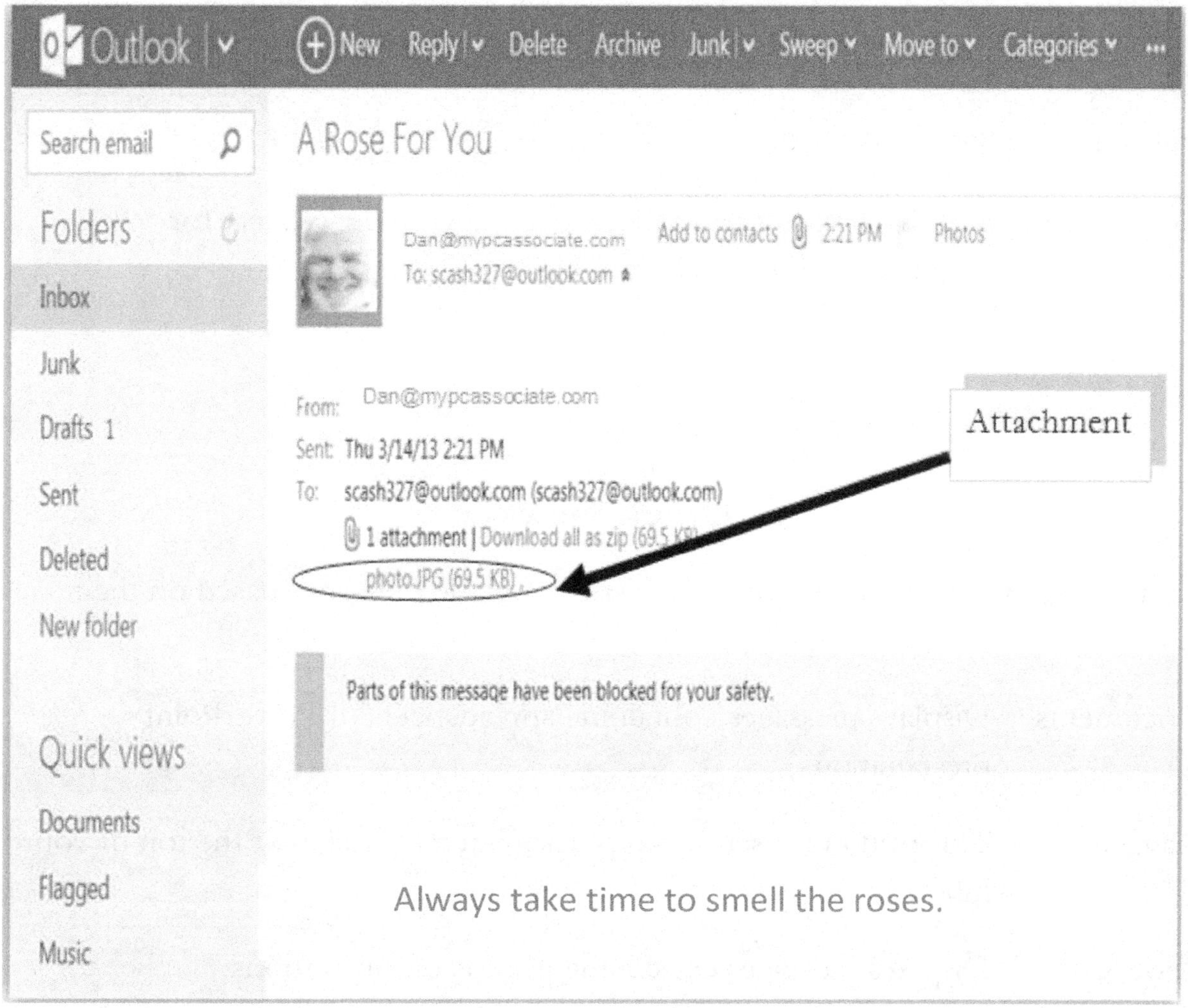

Figure 32

To open an attachment, click on the file name. The name of the attached file in Figure 32 is photo.jpg.

Microsoft Outlook Folders and Views

Inbox	Where all new messages appear
Archive	A folder used for old messages you wish to retain. They will no longer appear in your inbox.
Junk	A folder designed to retain messages you don't want.
Drafts	Unfinished messages are saved to this folder.
Sent	Copies of e-mail that you send to others are placed in this folder.
Deleted	This folder holds the messages you have deleted from your inbox.
New Folder	Use this link to create and name a new folder. Great for organizing your e-mail by subject or type.

Quick Views

These Quick Viewing options will display specific messages based on their content

Documents	Displays messages containing spreadsheets or PowerPoint presentations.
Flagged	This option is used to keep designated messages at the top of your inbox.
Photos	Displays messages containing photos or illustrations.
Shipping	Any messages containing tracking numbers for packages will appear in this view.
New Category	Use this link to create a customized view.

Printing and Saving E-Mail Messages

On occasion, you will find it useful to be able to print a copy of an e-mail message or attachment, and again this is fairly easy to do with Outlook.com.

To print an e-mail message, click on the Actions button, and then choose the Print message option. To print the attachment, you will need to click your left mouse button. When you are prompted, choose the Save option. This will save the attachment to your hard-drive. Open the attached file from your hard-drive and then print as usual.

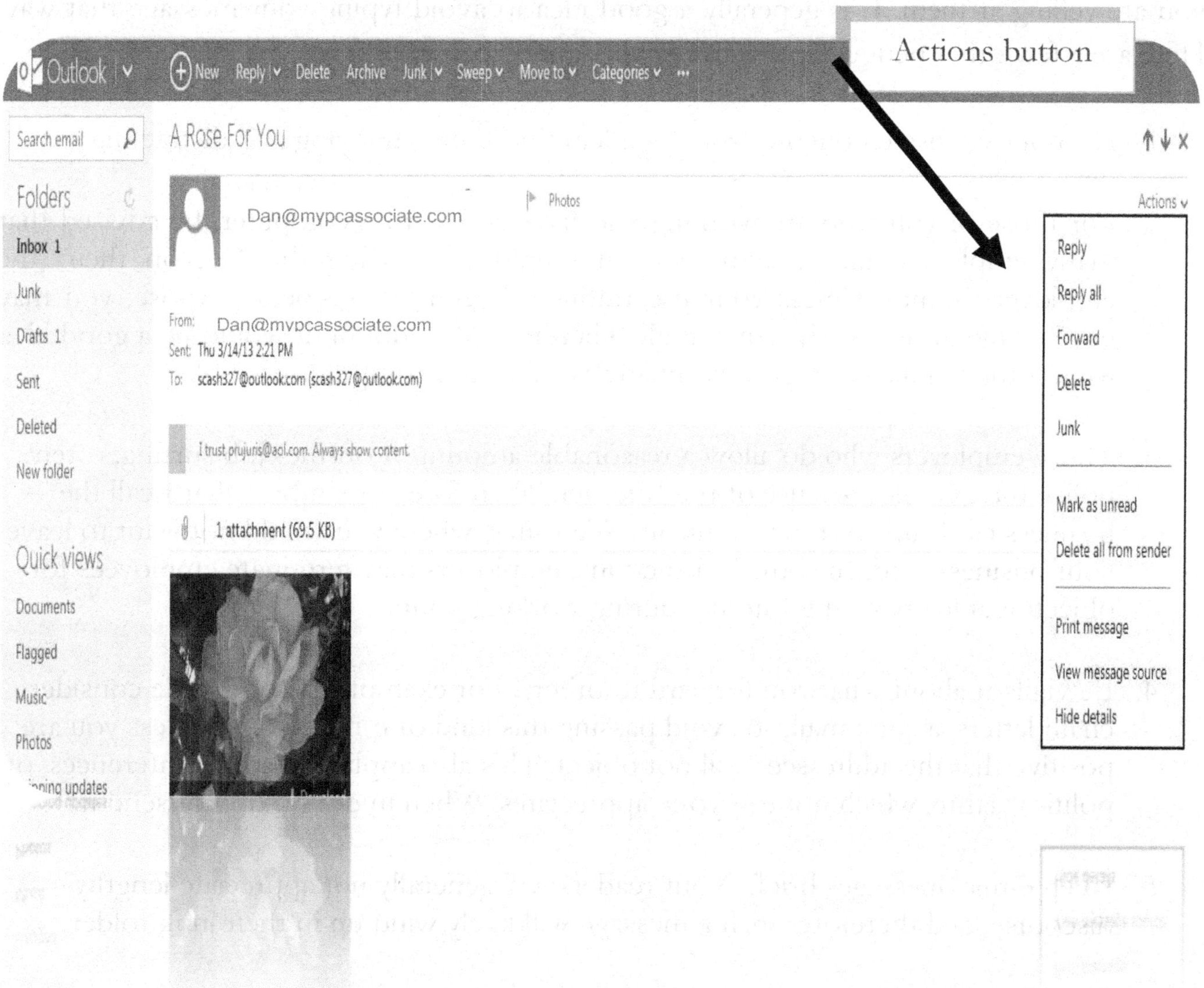

Figure 33

Practice Good Netiquette

Netiquette (Net Etiquette) has to do with how we conduct ourselves when we interact with others in Cyberspace. What do I mean by this? Well, keep in mind that when you send an e-mail, the recipient generally doesn't get to see you, and they can't observe your facial expressions or sense your sincerity. All they really have to go by are your words. If for example, you type your entire message in capital letters; your reader will feel as though you are yelling at them. It is generally a good idea to avoid typing your message that way. Here are a few other netiquette practices you should keep in mind.

1. Do not over use emoticons, some readers find them annoying and distracting.

2. For those of you who are working and have access to a computer, be advised that many employers take a dim view of employees surfing the Net on their (the employer's dime). Unless your use fulfills a legitimate business purpose, you may not be able to use the Internet at all. Therefore, if in doubt, it would be a good idea to become familiar with your company's e-mail and computer use policy.

3. Those employers who do allow a reasonable amount of on-the- job surfing, often police their employee's use of the Internet. Therefore, remember what I call the business card rule. Avoid visiting any Web sites, where you would not want to leave your business card. In some jurisdictions, employers may terminate employees for objectionable use of the Internet during working hours.

4. Be vigilant about what you forward to others. For example, many people consider chain letters as junk mail, so avoid passing this kind of e-mail along, unless you are positive that the addressees will not object. This also applies to sexual inferences, or political satire, which not everyone appreciates. When in doubt, do not send it.

5. Keep e-mail messages brief. Your readers will generally not appreciate lengthy discourse, and therefore, such a message will likely wind up in their junk folder.

6. Consider whether e-mail is really the most appropriate medium for your message. Disciplining employees, disagreement with your supervisor, co-workers, family or friends are examples of the types of communication best handled in person. Once you put something in writing and press the send button, the deed is done, and the message cannot be taken back.

Chapter Review Questions

1. Compose the following e-mail message **exactly** as it appears.

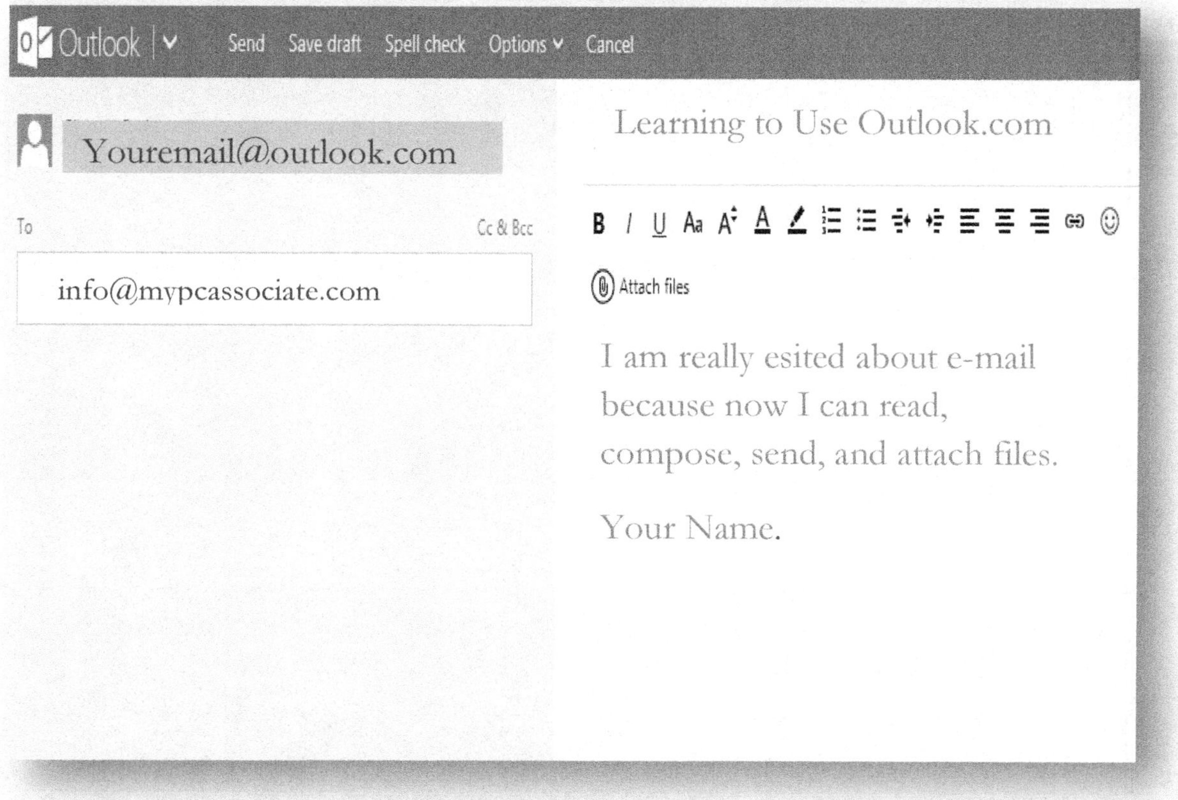

2. Place an emoticon at the end of your e-mail message.

3. Run the spell check program, if any errors were detected, correct them and then send the message. Notice that the word "esited" is misspelled.

4. When you receive a reply to your e-mail, print it out using the Outlook.com Actions button.

5. Explain the meaning of the business card rule.

My Notes:

Chapter 7

Keeping Safe on the Internet

- Describe the Threats to Online Security
- Identify Safeguards Against Viruses
- Describe the Safeguards Against Phishing and Identity theft
- Explain the Term Scareware
- Set Privacy Controls in Internet Explorer

Threats to Online Security and How to Keep Safe

Surfing the Web, shopping online, e-mailing family and liking friends on Facebook represents some of the many wonders the Internet has to offer. However, like just about any facet in life, there is a less than wonderful experience awaiting the unwary and uninitiated. So while we want you to enjoy the Internet, we also want you to be safe, and towards that end, it is important that you become acquainted with threats to your security online, and the fairly simple steps you can take to keep safe while you're out there surfing the Web.

To get started, here is a list of some new terms with which you should become familiar. While most terms will be explained in this chapter, others will appear in the glossary at the back of the book, and will contain more detailed explanations.

- Computer Virus
- Anti-virus software
- Phishing
- Scareware
- Identity theft
- Spam
- Scammers

Watch out for Viruses!

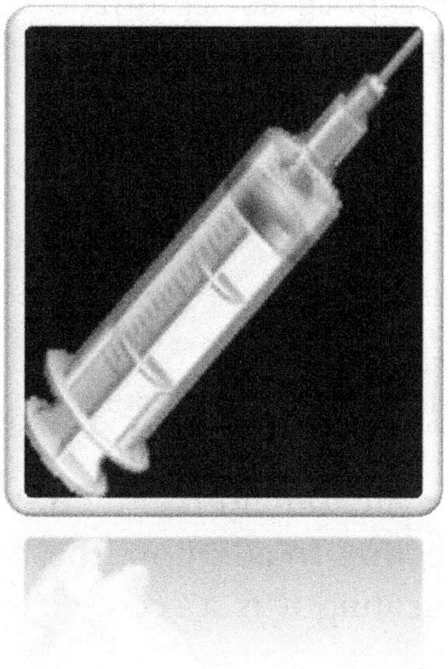

Believe it or not computers get viruses. While they are pretty immune to their owner's coughing and sneezing, unfortunately, they are pretty susceptible to the malicious work of a nefarious computer programmer. A computer programmer is a person who is generally paid to write software instructions or "code" that computers understand.

When an evil computer programmer writes bad code into a software program your computer can become infected, if you download or copy files from that computer. The program containing the bad "code" often includes instructions to perform some destructive task on your computer when the contaminated file is copied. Such instructions may actually cause the deletion or corruption of files on your computer.

Recommendation

Install a copy of anti-virus software on your computer. Well known anti-virus software programs include, Norton and McAfee. Contact your Internet Service Provider, (ISP) and inquire about whether they can make such software available to you. As a benefit, some ISPs offer it to their customers as a service. Others may charge a fee. Anti-virus software can also be purchased at most office supply stores, and the software is generally very affordable, though you will likely have to purchase updates. To protect against the risk of viruses, it is definitely worth it for you to have anti-virus software installed on your computer.

As a matter of good practice avoid opening e-mails from unfamiliar sources. Be advised that one way for your computer to get a virus is through e-mail attachments; **therefore, you should be very careful about opening attachments from unfamiliar sources.**

For New Computer Buyers

If you are purchasing a new computer, check to see if a trial version of anti-virus software comes with your software bundle. When the trial period expires, you will be prompted to purchase the software.

Phishing (Pronounced as Fishing)

Thieves think the Internet is a wonderful tool for assisting them with stealing the credit and personal information from "newbies" in particular. A newbie is someone who is new to the Internet. If that's you, be aware that would-be thieves may pose as legitimate businesses and even present legitimate looking Websites, hoping you will submit personal information that can be used to obtain goods and services. In other words, they are phishing.

Recommendation

Use trusted Websites for online purchases. When you are purchasing goods or services online, be sure that you are providing data to a secure website. You can tell if a site is secure by examining two locations on your screen. The address bar will contain the Web site's URL and will include http**s**: in the address; the "**s**" stands for secure. In addition, the lower-right hand corner of the Web site will display a tiny lock, indicating it is a secured site. When in doubt, do not provide personal or credit information online.

Avoid opening any e-mails that ask you to provide personal information, i.e. banking, credit card or Social Security numbers, passwords. Do not give out your username or password. **Reputable organizations do not ask for this information through e-mail**. If you believe you are being phished, you can report this activity to phishing-report@us-cert.gov

Phishing

From Wikipedia, the free online encyclopedia

Phishing is the act of attempting to acquire information such as usernames, passwords, and credit card details (and sometimes, indirectly, money) by masquerading as a trustworthy entity in an electronic communication. Communications purporting to be from popular social web sites, auction sites, online payment processors or IT administrators are commonly used to lure the unsuspecting public. Phishing emails may contain links to websites that are infected with malware.[1] Phishing is typically carried out by e-mail spoofing[2] or instant messaging,[3] and it often directs users to enter details at a fake

If you want to learn more, go online and try Wikipedia; it's is a great source of information.

Scareware

Armed with a computer and an Internet connection some thieves known as scammers, have created an entire industry out of scaring the unsuspecting Internet user. Though you can't see their faces, (and that's the point), they will use their computers to scare you into thinking there is something wrong with your computer. In other words they will perpetrate a scam by sending a phony message that will appear on your screen. They may offer you a free security scan that will help identify computer security threats. The message will then ask you to pay $30, $40 or $50 for software that will get rid of these so-called threats. The selling of so-called scareware is a common scam.

Recommendation

Scareware perpetrators may take great care in trying to look as polished and professional as possible, and that's half their battle. The other half is getting you to buy into their scam. Don't fall for it! **Do not** respond to any ad that attempts to pressure you to download security software. According to the Federal Trade Commission, when confronted with a scareware site, your best course of action is to shut down your browser. In other words, close Internet Explorer or Safari, etc. **Do not** click on the Windows close [**x**] button. **Do not click on "No" or "Cancel"**, as these may actually activate the very programs you are attempting to avoid."[2]

[2] Federal Trade Commission. "." . http://www.consumer.ftc.gov/articles/o263-free-security-scans (accessed March 15, 2013).

Identity Theft and Ways to Protect Against It

Identity theft occurs when someone steals your personal information and uses it to obtain goods or services in your name. The kinds of personal information thieves most often seek includes: credit cards, social security numbers, bank statements, etc. These thieves engage in a number of different tactics in order to obtain personal information. Such tactics include:

1. Dumpster diving. Some thieves will actually troll dumpsters and/or garbage cans, searching for enough tidbits of personal information to identify you and then impersonate you to banks, stores, etc.

2. Stealing a wallet or purse. Be aware that if your purse or wallet is stolen, thieves are no longer content to take the cash. They now likely have your credit card, driver's license, and ATM card. These items are sufficient for them to impersonate you.

3. Stealing your mail or submitting a change of address in your name. This is a common tactic for people engaging in identity theft. By routing your mail to another address they are able to purchase goods or services in your name.

Protecting Against Identity Theft Involves Being Proactive

If you want to deter identity theft you must be proactive. Here are a few dos and don'ts:

- **Do not walk around with your social security card in your wallet or purse**. Gone are the days when we were advised to keep it so handy. If your wallet or purse gets stolen you can deprive a would-be thief of a prime target, your Social Security number. Store your social security card in a safe place at home.

- **Don't use easy passwords** that someone who knows you can easily guess.

- **Don't give out personal information**, unless you are sure who you're dealing with. When in doubt, pick up the phone and contact the institution directly. This includes usernames, passwords, etc. .

- Avoid paying for goods or services online with your ATM/debit cards. Generally banks provide better protection to credit card holders.

- Create a separate PayPal account for online purchases. This vendor handles the purchase and sale of goods online, and your personal credit information is shielded from the seller. Always keep printouts of your online purchases.

- Do get a shredder. It's no longer sufficient to just tear monthly bills in half. It is very important that you shred documents that contain personal information. Such information also includes credit applications, credit offers and insurance forms.

- Do keep your information secure- if you have to write down passwords, and who doesn't these days, place them in a secure location.

- Do monitor your credit report. You are entitled to one free credit report from each of the credit reporting agencies once a year. It's a good idea to monitor your report for any signs of identity theft. If you do believe you are the victim of identity theft, report it to your bank, and the credit reporting agencies immediately.

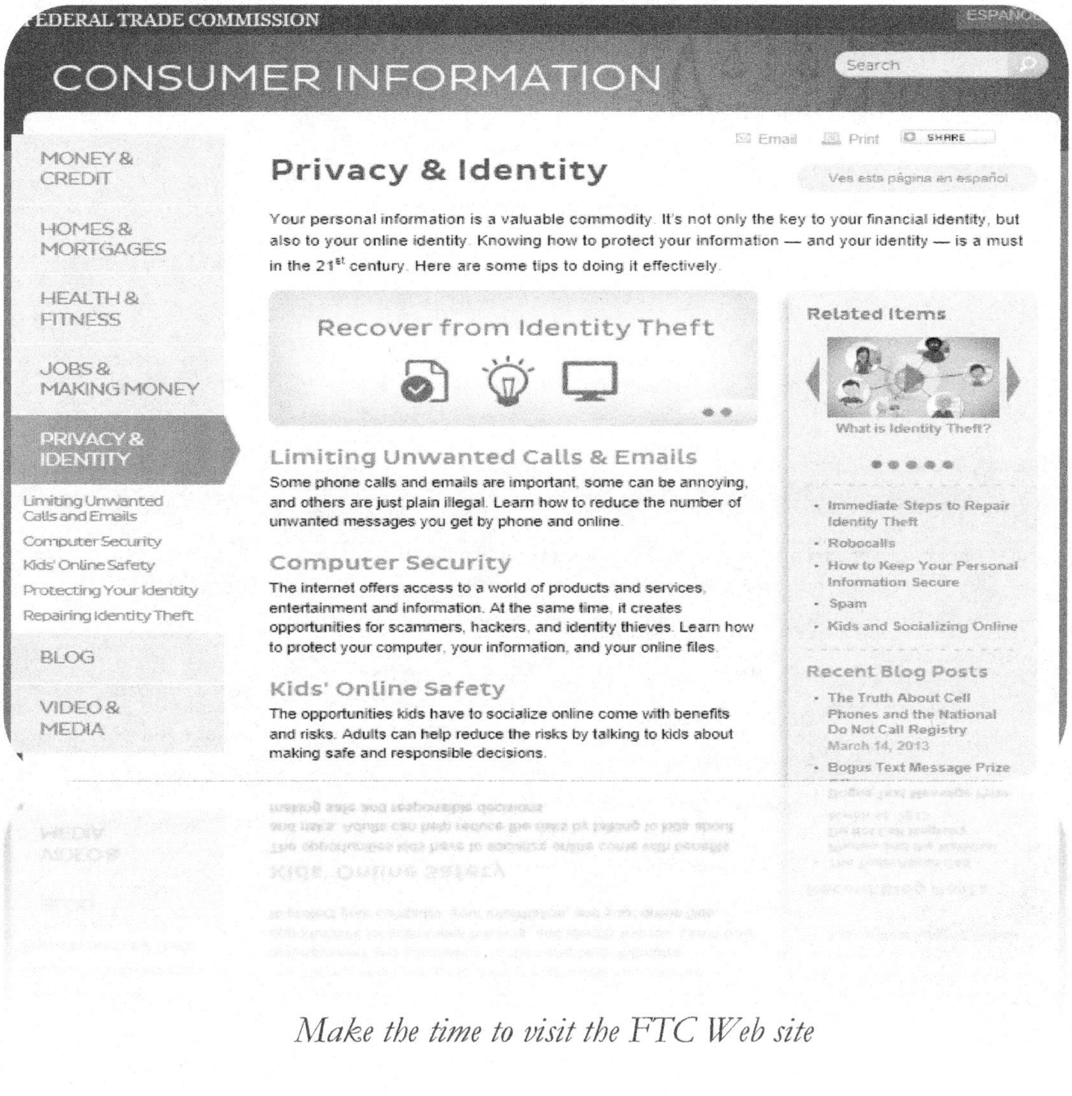

Make the time to visit the FTC Web site

Setting Privacy Controls in Internet Explorer

Internet users are becoming increasingly concerned about their privacy. When you visit a Web site, some companies may place a "cookie" on your computer. A "cookie" is a tiny file that collects information about your preferences.

Vendors generally use these preferences to market goods and/or services to you based on prior visits to their Web sites. For example, suppose you purchase a mystery at Web site A in January. In March when you visit the site again, several new mystery books may be suggested, and ads for them will pop up on your screen. This happens because a "cookie" stored your preference for these types of books and instructed site A to display new books of this type to you. The assumption is of course that you will appreciate this kind of attention.

If this kind of marketing makes you a little queasy, then you will probably appreciate Internet Explorer's safe browsing options. Internet Explorer makes several privacy options available to you through its Safety menu. To delete cookies follow these steps:

1. Click on the Tools menu
2. Select the Safety option
3. Select the Delete browsing history menu option
4. Select the Cookies check box and then click on the Delete button

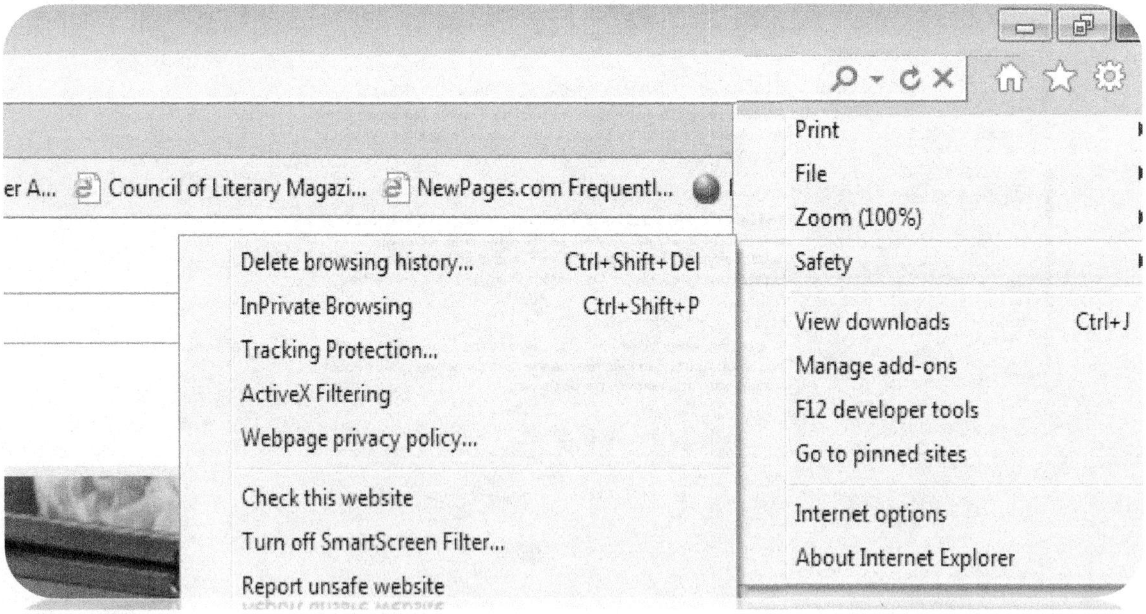

Figure 34

The Delete Browsing History Dialog Box

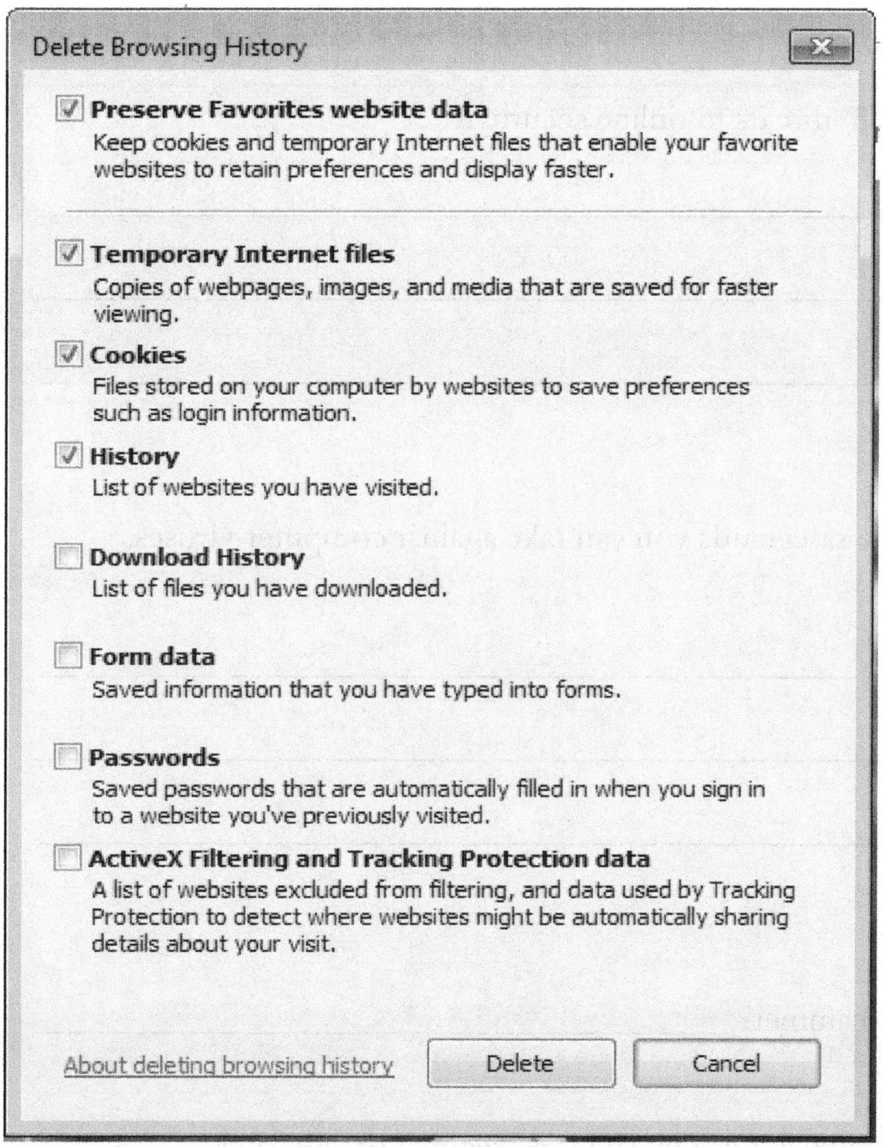

Figure 35

You can modify several privacy settings from the Delete browsing history dialog box. To learn more about this feature, click on the About deleting browsing history link. This link is located in the lower left-hand corner of the delete browsing history dialog box.

Chapter Review Questions

1. List three (3) threats to online security.

a)____

b)____

c)____

2. Identify the safeguards you can take against computer viruses.

a)____

b)____

c)____

3. What is a scammer? ____________________________

4. How can you tell if a Web site is a "secure" or safe site?

5. List at least three steps you can take to prevent identity theft.

a)____

b)____

c)____

My Notes:

My Notes:

Appendices

Appendix A

Answers to the Chapter Review Questions

Chapter 1

1. Three benefits made possible by computer networks are: a) file sharing, b) reducing costs and c) communications.

2. The term used to describe the selling of goods and services online is e-commerce.

3. Some of the activities that can be performed on the Internet include: a) emailing, b) shopping, c) researching information, d) selling a home or business, e) booking a vacation. Of course, this is not an exhaustive list.

4. The word LAN stands for local area network. A LAN is created by connecting a group of computers together in the same building.

5. The word WAN stands for wide area network. A WAN is a network that extends beyond a single building.

Chapter 2

1. The requirements for establishing an Internet connection include: a) a personal computer, b) a network interface card, c) a phone connection, d) a router e) a browser program, like Internet Explorer, and f) an Internet Service Provider.

2. Internet service providers make it possible for their customers to connect to the Internet. Customers are provided with usernames and passwords.

3. A browser is a software program that makes it possible for a user to view hypermedia, i.e., Web pages that include links, graphics and text.

4. Common domain extensions include: a) .com, .edu, .and .org. Other extensions include .net, and .co

Chapter 3

1. Entering the URL: www.disney.com will take you to the Walt Disney Theme Park Web site.

2. Yes, there are several pictures on this Web site.

3. Some of the pictures are actually links.

4. Some of the links on this Web page include: a) TV, b) Music, c) Video, d) Games.

5. Entering the URL: www.google.com will take you to the Google search engine page.

6. Typing the search terms "Internet Dictionary" will cause Google to search for every occurrence of the word Internet Dictionary in its index.

7. You should see no less than 401,000,000 results (0.18 seconds) as of 3/2013.

Chapter 4

1. In this exercise you are required to visit the aarp.org Web site, and then perform the following task:

    a) Launch Internet Explorer.

    b) In the address field, type: www.aarp.org.

    c) Click on the Tools button, and choose Print.

    d) Select Print.

    e) Choose OK to send your document to the printer.

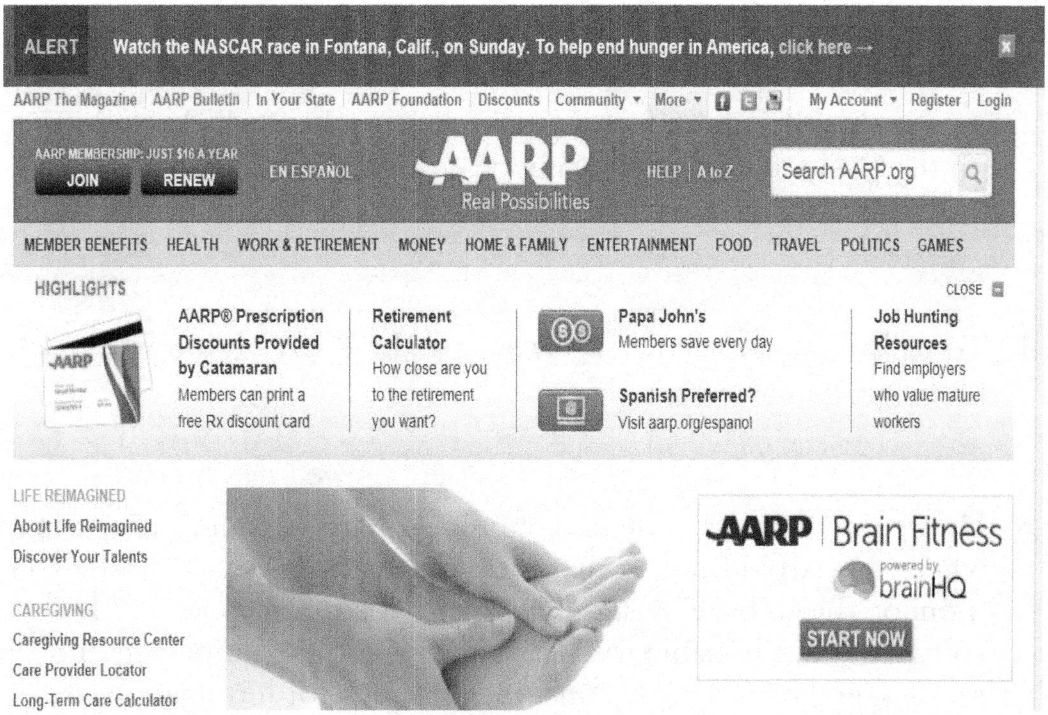

2. To place an emoticon in your e-mail message, simply click on the little smiley face located on the Outlook.com toolbar.

3. To run the spell checking program, click on the Spell check button located on the Outlook toolbar. See above.

4. To reply to an e-mail message, click on the Reply button while viewing the message you received.

5. Under the business card rule, employees are encouraged not to visit sites where they would not want to leave their business card. Many employers monitor the websites visited by employees during working hours. Visiting so-called objectionable sites are disturbing to employers for legitimate reasons, and may actually constitute grounds for termination.

Chapter 6

1. Threats to online security include, among others:

   a) Viruses.

   b) Phishing.

   c) Identity Theft.

2. Safeguards you can take against computer viruses include:

   a) Using anti-virus software.

   b) Avoid downloading files from questionable sites.

   c) Not opening attachments when you don't know the source.

3. A scammer is someone who uses their compute to pose as a legitimate Web site with the intent to obtain personal information.

4. You can tell if a Web site is secure by looking for "https" in its address, and by looking for the lock icon.

5. To prevent identity theft, Internet users are advised to:

   a) Avoid carrying a Social Security Card.

   b) Avoid giving out personal information, like usernames and passwords.

   c) Monitor their credit reports.

   d) Use a shredder when discarding bills or bank statements.

   e) Avoid paying online with debit cards, use a credit card instead.

Appendix B

Interesting Online Resources for -Seniors

1.	www.seniorplanet.org	Activities, resources for seniors
2.	Aarp.org	Advocacy, resources
3.	Medicare.gov	Informational resources - government
4.	Socialsecurity.gov	Informational resources - government
5.	Seniornet.org	Activities, resources for seniors
6.	Olderpeoplesday.co.uk/	United Kingdom
7.	Webmd.com	General medical information
8.	Aoa.gov	U.S. Administration on Aging
9.	Uwo.ca/actage	Canadian Centre for Activity & Aging

Some U.S. Internet Service Providers

Check your local telephone directory for additional listings in your area

1.	Aol.com	ISP
2.	Comcast.com	Cable TV, ISP
3.	Prodigy.com	ISP
4.	Directv.com	Cable TV, ISP
5.	Verizon.net	TV, ISP
6.	TimeWarnerCable.com	Cable TV, ISP
7.	Netzero.com	Internet
8.	Earthlink.com	Internet
9.	www.attspecial.com/At&t_Internet	ISP

Popular Social Media Web Sites

1.	Facebook.com	Social networking
2.	Myspace.com	Social networking
3.	Linkedin.com	Business networking
4.	Twitter.com	Micro blogging, social networking
5.	Badoo.com	European social networking site
6.	Migente.com	Latin American social networking site
7.	Trulycaribbean.net	Caribbean social networking
8.	Goodreads.com	Literary/Books

Popular Search Engines

1. Google.com
2. Bing.com
3. Lycos.com
4. Altavista.com
5. AOLsearch.com
6. Yahoo.com
7. Ask.com
8. Excite.com
9. msn.com
10. Baidu.com

Examples of News and Entertainment Web Sites

1.	Movietickets.com	Movies
2.	Moviefone.com	Movies
3.	Movies.yahoo.com	Movies
4.	Youtube.com	Videos
5.	Itunes.com	Music
6.	Hulu.com	TV
7.	Nytimes.com	New York Times
8.	Cnn.com	Cable News Network
9.	Pbs.org/	Public Broadcasting Service
10.	Global.nytimes.com/?iht	International Herald Tribune
11.	Huffingpost.com	Huffington Post
12.	Thetimes.co.uk/	The London Times
13.	amsterdamnews.com/	Amsterdam News (NYC)

Popular Online Shopping Websites

1.	Amazon.com	Merchandise, books, etc.
2.	Barnesandnoble.com	Books
3.	Macys.com	Merchandise
4.	Ebay.com	Auction
5.	Itunes.com	Music
6.	Homedepot.com	Hardware
7.	Ticketron.us	Broadway tickets, etc.
8.	Bestbuy.com	Electronics, appliances, etc.
9.	UPS.com	Mail and package delivery
10.	FedEx.com	Mail and package delivery
11.	HSN.com	Merchandise
12.	QVC.com	Merchandise

Some Educational Websites of Interest

Note: Some of the institutions listed below offer Massive Open Online Courses (MOOCs) MOOCs do not generally offer degree programs. If you are interested in short-term non-degree educational programs, a MOOC may be a good fit for you. You may also want to consider schools known for their online educational programs. Finally, consider courses offered by your local college or university. Many schools offer students of all ages the ability to take distance-learning classes.

1.	Cosera	MOOC	https://www.coursera.org/courses
2.	edX	MOOC	https://www.edx.org/
3.	Udacity	MOOC	https://www.udacity.com
4.	Udemy	MOOC	https://www.udemy.com/
5.	Course Hero	MOOC	http://www.coursehero.com
6.	Capitol College	Offers online courses	http://www.capitol-college.edu
7.	University of Phoenix	Offers online courses and degrees	http://www.phoenix.edu
8.	Walden University	Offers online courses	http://www.waldenu.edu
9.	Argosy University	Offers online courses	http://www.argosy.edu
10.	Colorado State University	Offers online courses	http://www.colostate.edu

Appendix C

Keeping Track of Your Internet Accounts

If you become an avid fan of the Internet, then you will no doubt accumulate a number of online accounts. Whether you are purchasing goods or services, vendors will likely require that you create user accounts as a prerequisite. This means that you will have to keep track of all of your usernames and passwords.

For security reasons, it is not a good idea to use the same username and password for all of your accounts. Since you will never remember all of the account names you have set-up, consider storing your passwords and user accounts in a safe and convenient place.

Appendix C

E-Mail Address Directory

Keep track of your family, friends, cyber-pals, and websites with this handy directory.

My E-Mail Address: ____

Family E-Mail

Name:	E-Mail Address:

My Friends

Name:	E-Mail Address:

My Cyber-Pals

Name:	E-Mail Address:

My Favorite Websites

Name:	Website Address:

Glossary of Popular Internet Terms

INFORMATION
HIGHWAY

Glossary of Popular Internet Terms

Anti-virus software: A software program Designed to identify, locate, and eliminate a computer virus otherwise known as bad or malicious code. Two of the most popular brands of anti-virus software include Norton and McAfee.

ARPA Net: Also known as the Advanced Research Projects Agency. ARPA developed packet-switching technology and the Transfer Protocol/Internet Protocol. during the 1960s which made it possible for dissimilar computers/networks to communicate, and which transformed the way data packets are distributed within a network.

Attachments: Files such as documents, photographs, music that can be attached to e-mail messages.

Backbone network: Generally refers to a central network to which many routers connect. Many organizations that set up their own WANs and LANs refer to them as backbones.

Blog: A kind of electronic journal or article that is generally published online and shared with others. Blogs can cover any number of subjects.

Bookmark: A software feature that permits an Internet user to mark a visited Web site. This causes the user's browser to record that Web site's address so the user does not have to retype it on a subsequent visit. See also Favorites, an Internet Explorer feature.

Bricks and mortar : The term used to describe a physical store or actual business as opposed to a "virtual" one.

Browser: A software program designed to facilitate the viewing of Internet resources such as Web pages.

Cookies: Small files deposited on an Internet user's computer. Cookies are generally designed to collect user preferences for the purpose of enhancing the marketing of goods and services.

Cyberspace: The term used to describe communication within the Internet environment. This includes the abundant resources available within the environment.

Domain names: The unique name that identifies an Internet site. Business domain names are often reminiscent of the company's trade name or service mark.

Downloading: The act of copying files from a server or remote computer to the local resources of an end-user, i.e. hard-drive, flash drive, CD.

E-Commerce: The term used to describe the buying and selling of goods via the Internet.

E-mail: Stands for electronic mail- A method for sending electronic messages to people using computers. Generally requires that users subscribe to an e-mail service.

E-mail address: A unique address assigned to an e-mail account holder.

Emoticon: A small symbol or image that represents an emotion. ☺ They are often used in e-mail or text messages.

Facebook.com: A popular social networking Web site. Developed by Mark Zuckerberg. It was initially designed to provide a forum for socializing and sharing common interest among friends and family but has grown to be substantially more since its inception. It also provides a forum and means of advertising.

FAQ: Frequently Asked Questions or FAQs for short are generally included on a variety of web pages and used to provide a means of supplying answers to questions about a product, or service. They are generally listed in question answer format.

Favorites: The term used to describe a folder in Microsoft's Internet Explorer. Previously visited Website addresses may be saved here for future reference.

Google.com : A search engine developed by Google Inc. Google is designed to enable users to search and retrieve documents and images containing key terms.

HTTP: Stands for hypertext transfer protocol (HTTP). The set of rules used to connect World Wide Web sites across the Internet. HTTPS means it's a secure site.

Hypertext Markup Language: Also referred to as HTML for short. HTML is a computer language used to create Web pages.

Identity theft: The intentional taking, misappropriation, and impersonation of another for the purpose of illegally obtaining goods and/or services.

Information highway: The term used to describe the Internet and its vast digital resources.

Instant messaging: A feature often provided by social networking and/or ISP services that permit users to exchange quick text-based messages to one another over the Internet. Also known as chatting.

Internet: The global internetworking of computers.

Internet Explorer: Microsoft Corporation's Internet browser program.

LAN (Local Area Network): A group of computers connected together within a single building or floor for the purpose of sharing files, facilitating communication and reducing costs.

Netiquette: The term used to describe the etiquette an Internet user ought to practice. Generally consists of a set of guidelines for communicating or interacting with others in Cyberspace.

Network: A group of computers connected together for the purpose of sharing resources, reducing costs, and providing some measure of security. There are different types of computer networks; see for example, LANs and WANs.

Network interface card (NIC): A device (actually a circuit board) that acts as an interface between one's computer and the network in which it must communicate. The NIC is what permits computers to join an active network.

Password: A unique set of characters generally chosen by a computer user to authenticate their identity to a computer network.

Router: A device or software program that handles the connection between two or more networks.

Scareware: The term used to describe a scam, in which the perpetrator attempts to convince an Internet user that their computer is in jeopardy and is subject to a security breach unless they purchase the scammer's software.

Search engine: A software program designed to facilitate the indexing, searching, and retrieval of information from Internet computers.

Server: A computer that can share and distribute resources such as software programs to "client" computers.

Social media: The term used to collectively refer to social networking websites.

Spam: Also referred to as spamming. It is the act of sending junk mail to Internet users through their e-mail accounts.

Twitter.com: Social networking and micro blogging Website. Tweeting is the act of sending out to others short messages or "tweets" consisting of no more than about 140 characters.

Universal resource locator (URL): The standard way to cite the address of any resource on the Internet that is part of the World Wide Web.

User name: The term used to describe or identify an individual on a network.

Virus: A computer program designed to invade a user's computer, and which is can be both disruptive and destructive in nature.

WAN (Wide Area Network): Any network that covers an area larger than a single building.

Website: A computer attached to the Internet supported by a server that makes content available to browsers. A collection of Web pages make up a Website.

WI-FI: The term used to describe the technology (actually a networking standard) which permits electronic devices to connect to and communicate with wireless networks. Wi-Fi enabled devices such as smart phones, tablets and computers include interface controllers that permit them to connect to wireless networks using radio waves as opposed to physical cables.

Wikipedia: Sometimes referred to as Wiki for short. It is in effect an Internet encyclopedia founded by Jimmy Wales. It is considered a community project in that individual Internet users are invited to contribute to its knowledgebase.

World Wide Web (WWW): The term used to describe the collection of hypertext servers.

Yahoo.com: A popular Internet corporation known for its search engine and e-mail facilities.

YouTube.com: The name of a popular Website which permits users to post and share video content.

Index

Index

O

P

Q

R

S

Table of Figures

About the Author

Diane Martin is executive director of My PC Associate NYC. She has been teaching computer applications in the fields of business and higher education since 1981. In 1999, with a background in business and legal technology, Diane migrated to the field of higher education, becoming the director of computer networking and support for a college of business and technology in New York City. Diane is a member of the Association of Information Technology Professionals. She is the author of "Office in a Minute: Steps for Performing Basic Tasks in Microsoft Office 2010" and "Office in a Minute: Steps for Performing Basic Tasks in Microsoft Office 2013."

In addition to a Juris Doctor degree, Diane also holds a Master of Science degree in Instructional Technology from New York Institute of Technology, and a Bachelor of Arts degree in Liberal Arts from Long Island University. She is a certified Senior Professional in Human Resources, (SPHR), and a certified Microsoft Office Specialist.

My Notes:

My Notes:

My Notes:

My Notes:

My Notes:

My Notes:

Made in the USA
Monee, IL
08 November 2026

67971937R00077